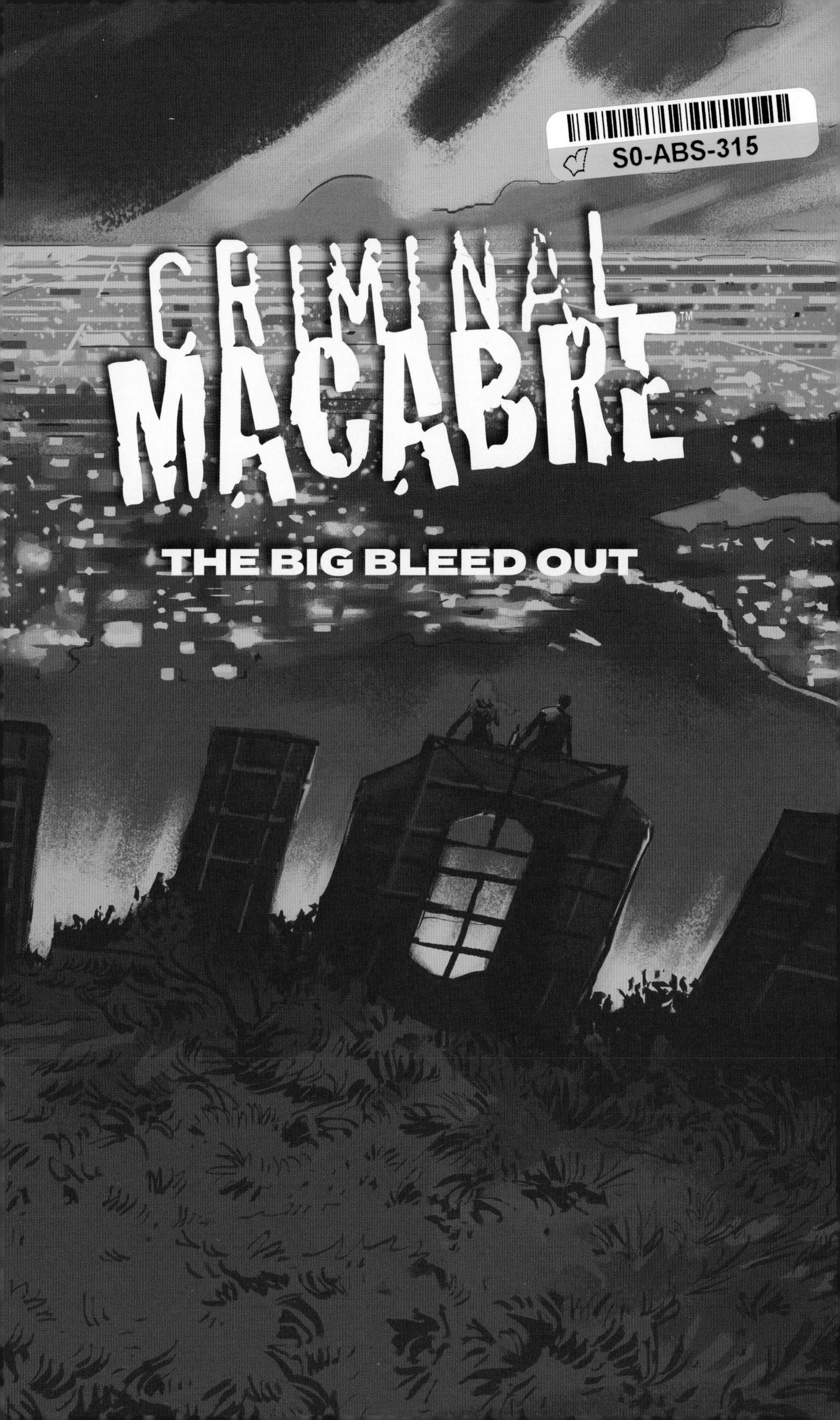
CRIMINAL
MACABRE™
THE BIG BLEED OUT

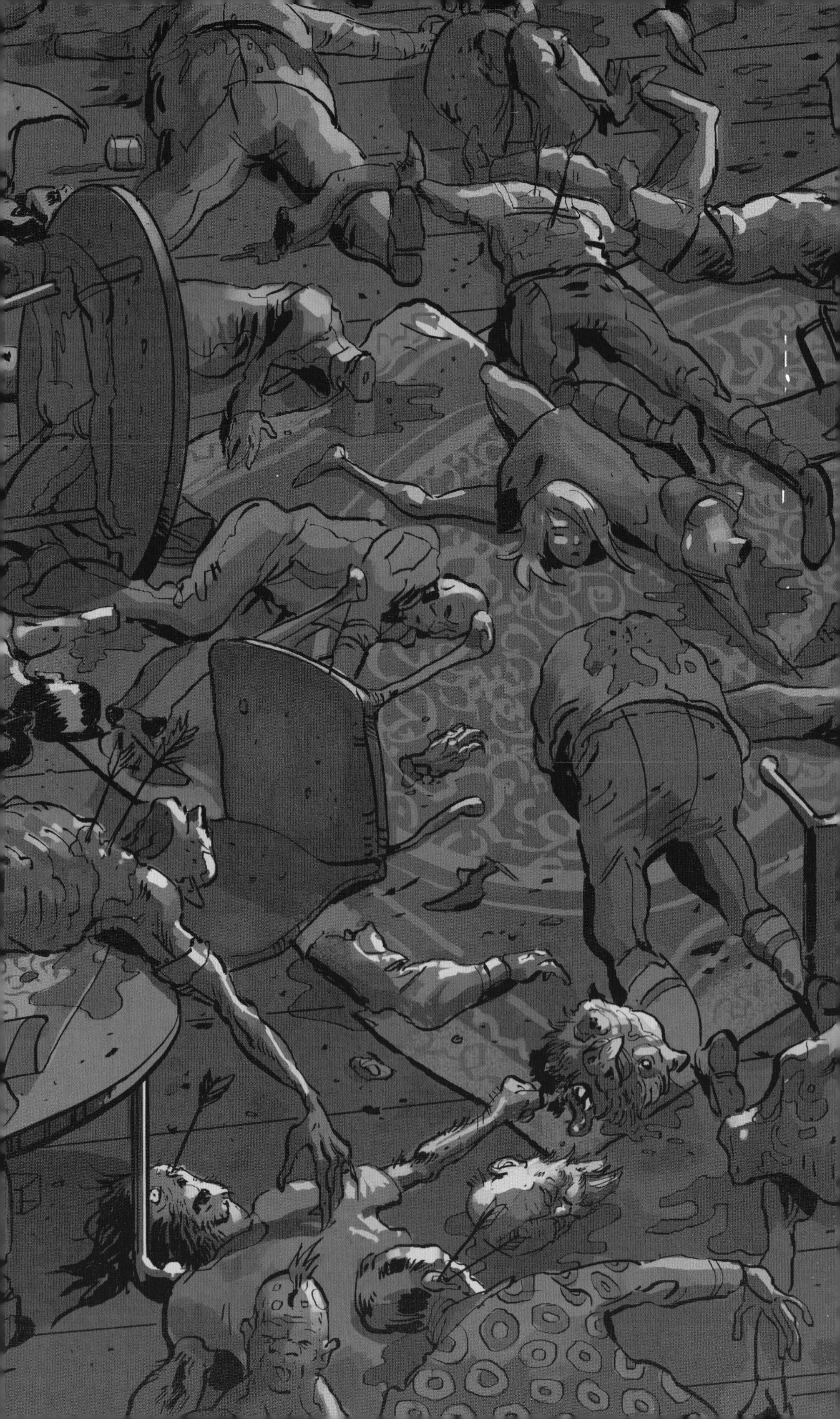

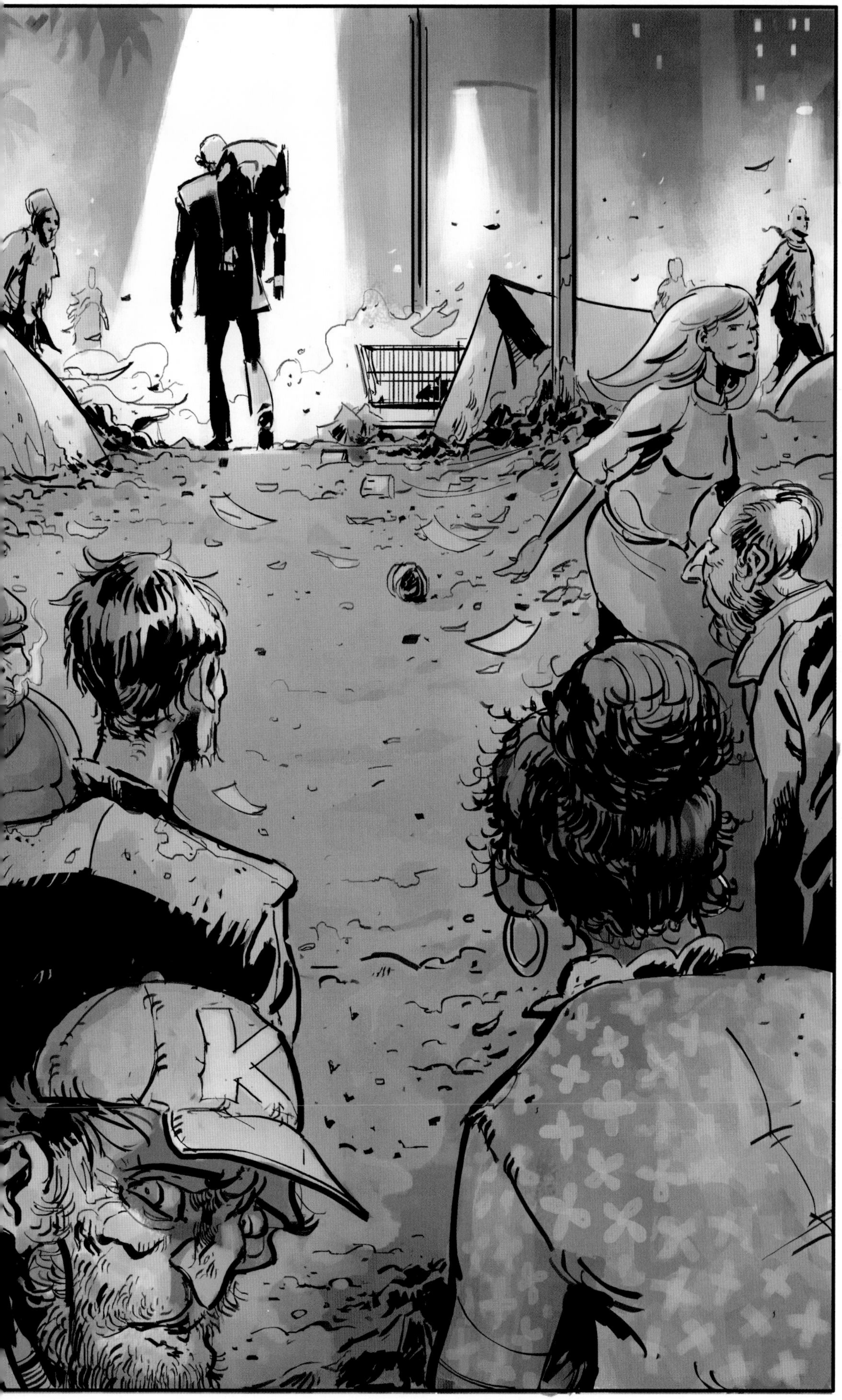

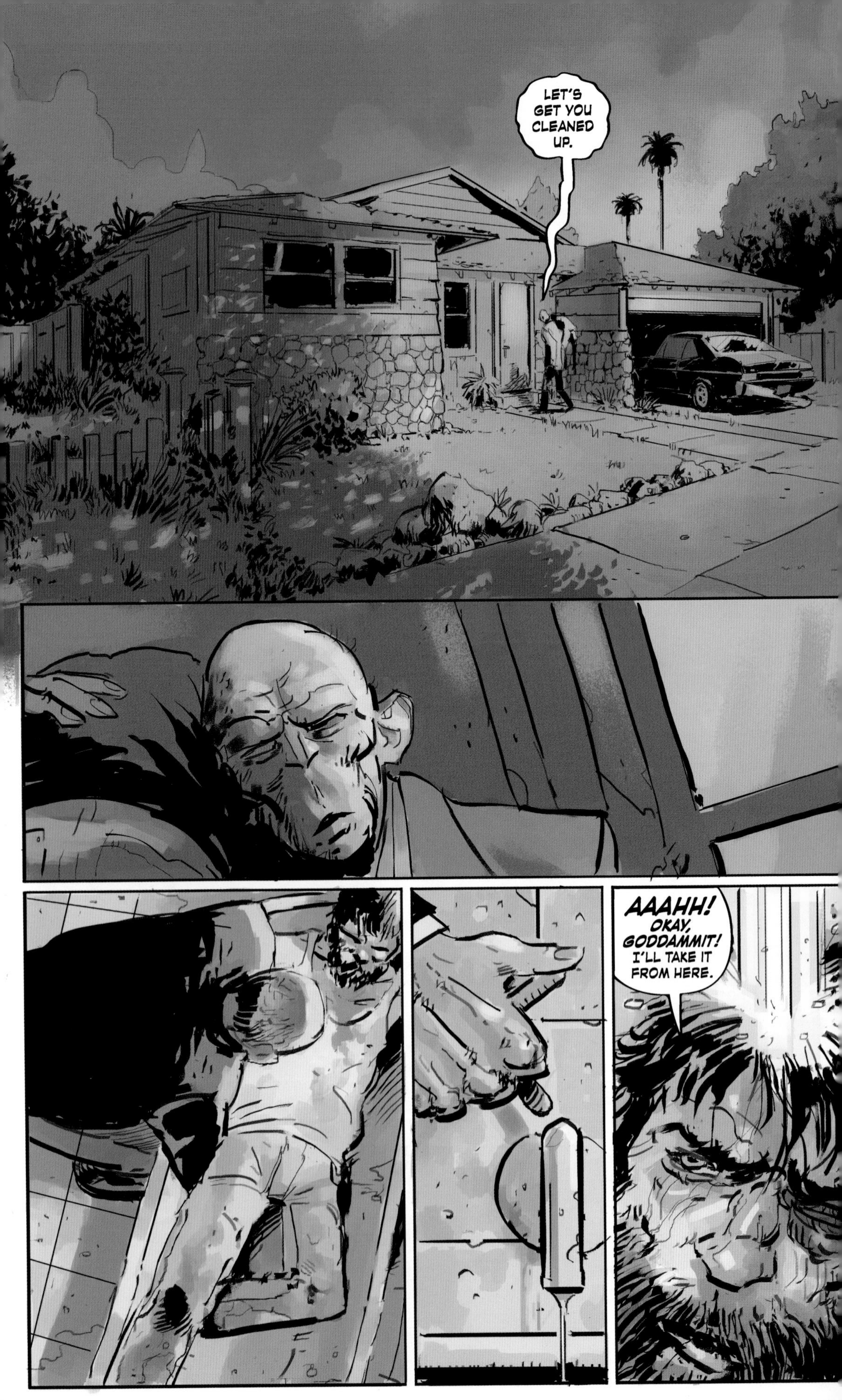
LET'S GET YOU CLEANED UP.
AAAHH! OKAY, GODDAMMIT! I'LL TAKE IT FROM HERE.

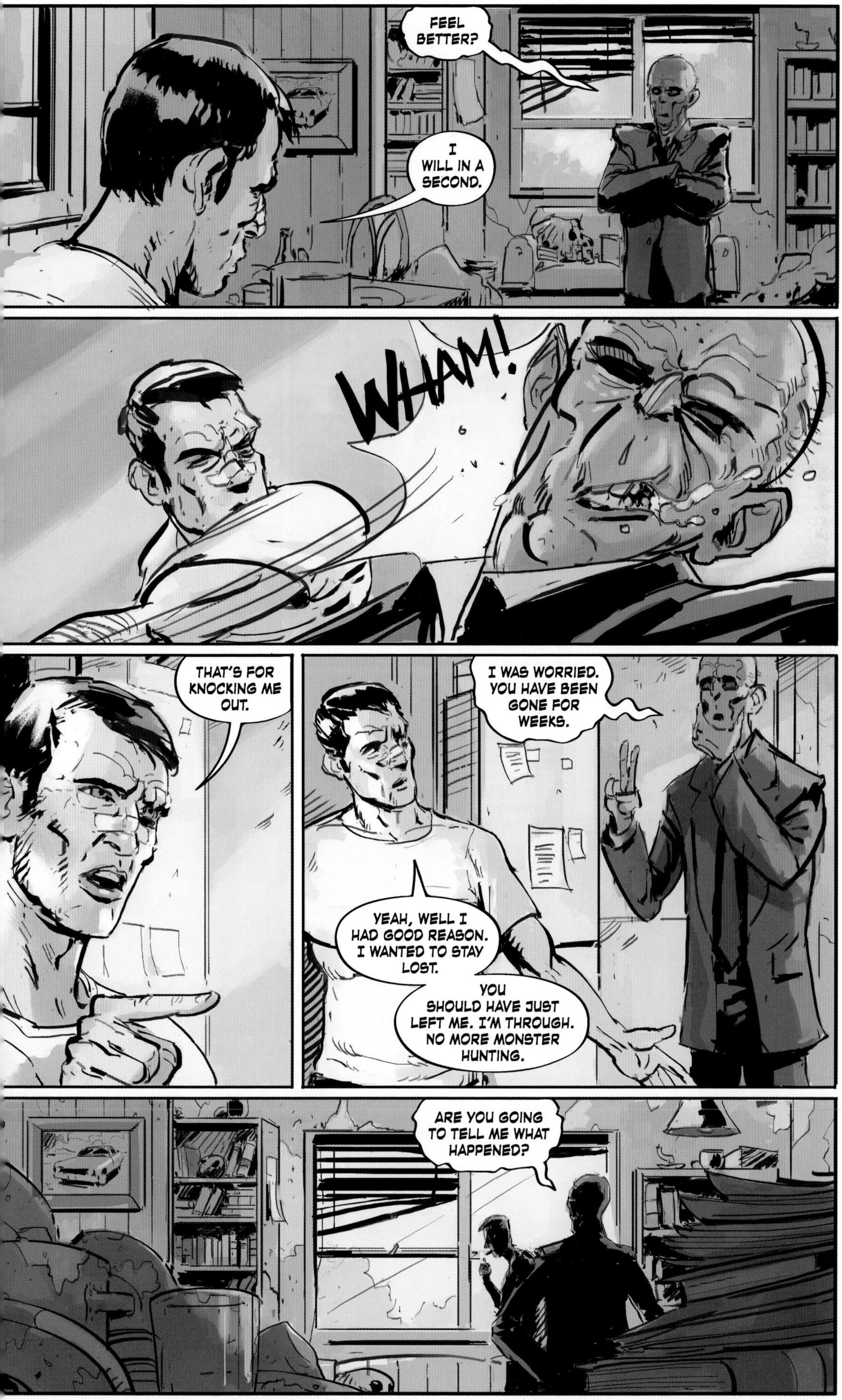
FEEL BETTER?
I WILL IN A SECOND.
WHAM!
THAT'S FOR KNOCKING ME OUT.
I WAS WORRIED. YOU HAVE BEEN GONE FOR WEEKS.
YEAH, WELL I HAD GOOD REASON. I WANTED TO STAY LOST.
YOU SHOULD HAVE JUST LEFT ME. I'M THROUGH. NO MORE MONSTER HUNTING.
ARE YOU GOING TO TELL ME WHAT HAPPENED?

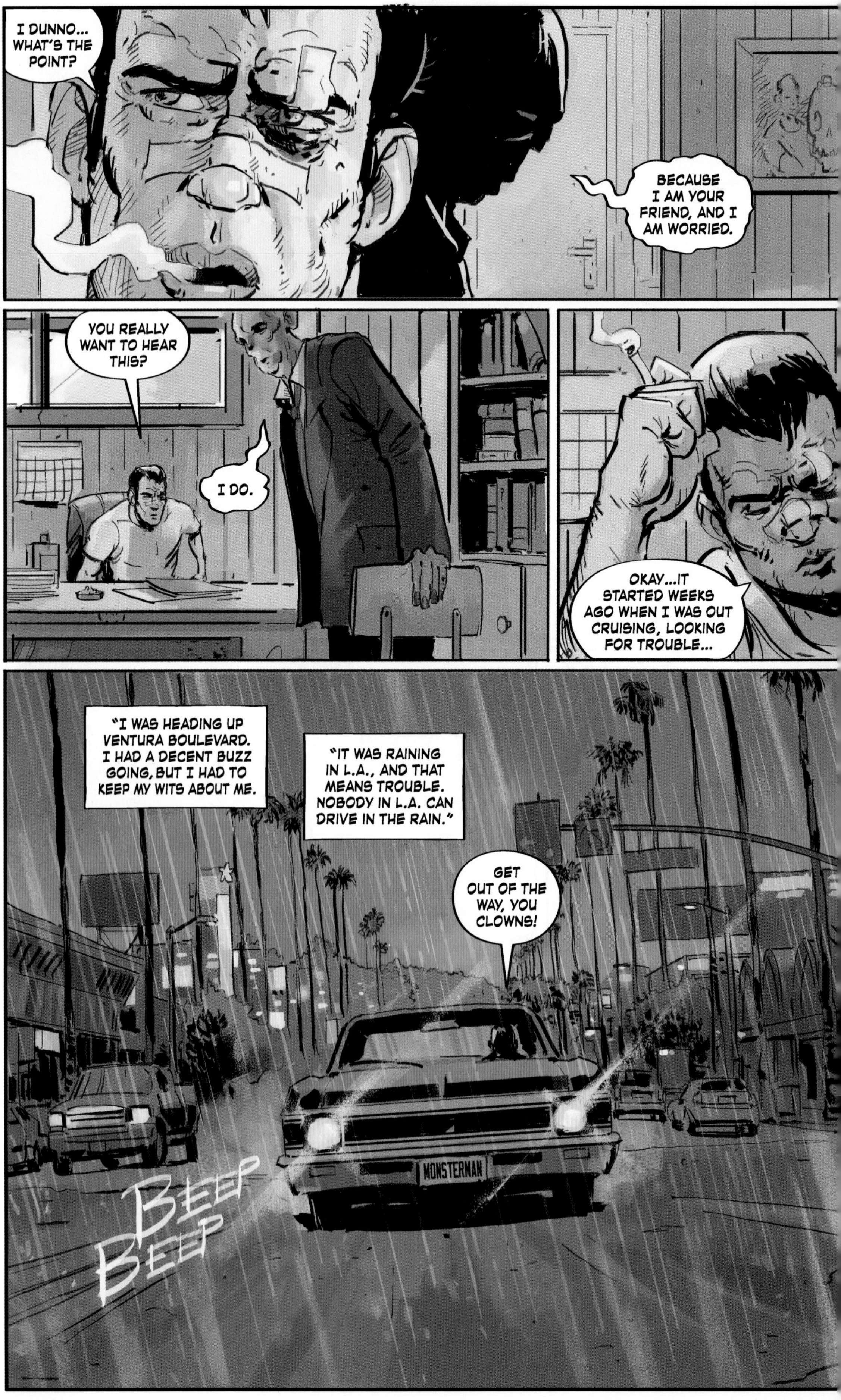
I DUNNO... WHAT'S THE POINT?
BECAUSE I AM YOUR FRIEND, AND I AM WORRIED.
YOU REALLY WANT TO HEAR THIS?
I DO.
OKAY...IT STARTED WEEKS AGO WHEN I WAS OUT CRUISING, LOOKING FOR TROUBLE...
"I WAS HEADING UP VENTURA BOULEVARD. I HAD A DECENT BUZZ GOING, BUT I HAD TO KEEP MY WITS ABOUT ME.
"IT WAS RAINING IN L.A., AND THAT MEANS TROUBLE. NOBODY IN L.A. CAN DRIVE IN THE RAIN."
GET OUT OF THE WAY, YOU CLOWNS!
MONSTERMAN
BEEP BEEP

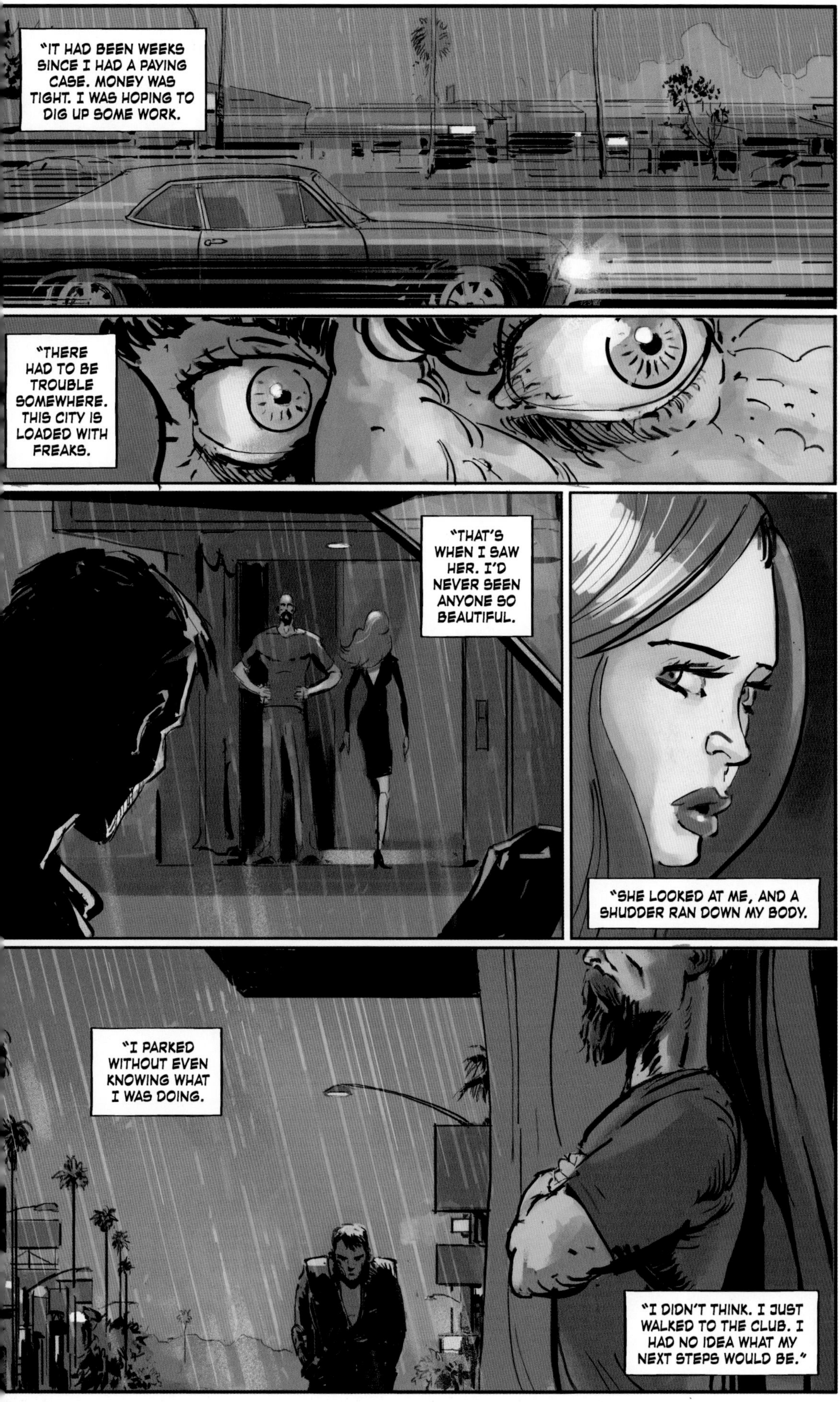
"IT HAD BEEN WEEKS SINCE I HAD A PAYING CASE. MONEY WAS TIGHT. I WAS HOPING TO DIG UP SOME WORK.
"THERE HAD TO BE TROUBLE SOMEWHERE. THIS CITY IS LOADED WITH FREAKS.
"THAT'S WHEN I SAW HER. I'D NEVER SEEN ANYONE SO BEAUTIFUL.
"SHE LOOKED AT ME, AND A SHUDDER RAN DOWN MY BODY.
"I PARKED WITHOUT EVEN KNOWING WHAT I WAS DOING.
"I DIDN'T THINK. I JUST WALKED TO THE CLUB. I HAD NO IDEA WHAT MY NEXT STEPS WOULD BE."

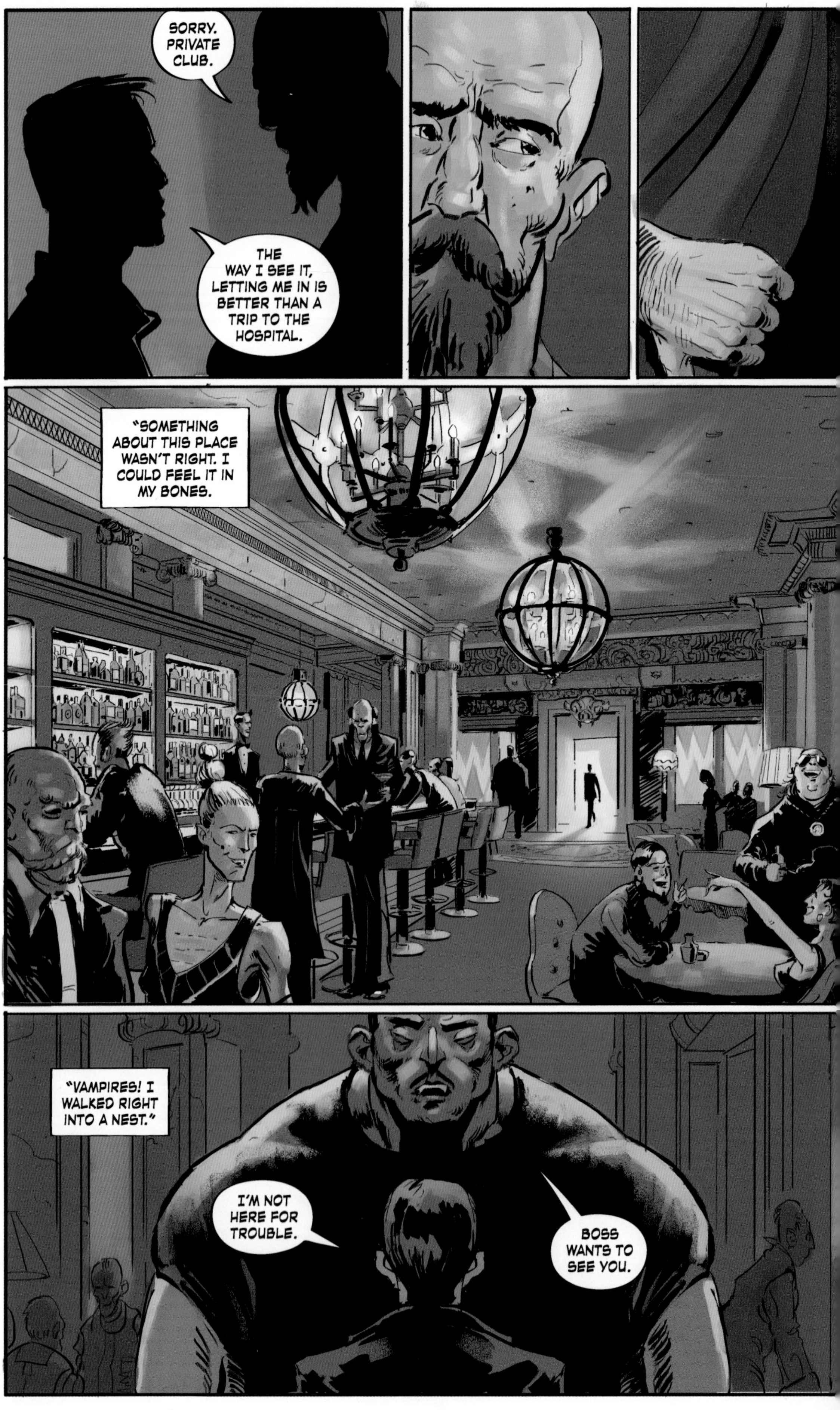
SORRY. PRIVATE CLUB.
THE WAY I SEE IT, LETTING ME IN IS BETTER THAN A TRIP TO THE HOSPITAL.
"SOMETHING ABOUT THIS PLACE WASN'T RIGHT. I COULD FEEL IT IN MY BONES.
"VAMPIRES! I WALKED RIGHT INTO A NEST."
I'M NOT HERE FOR TROUBLE.
BOSS WANTS TO SEE YOU.

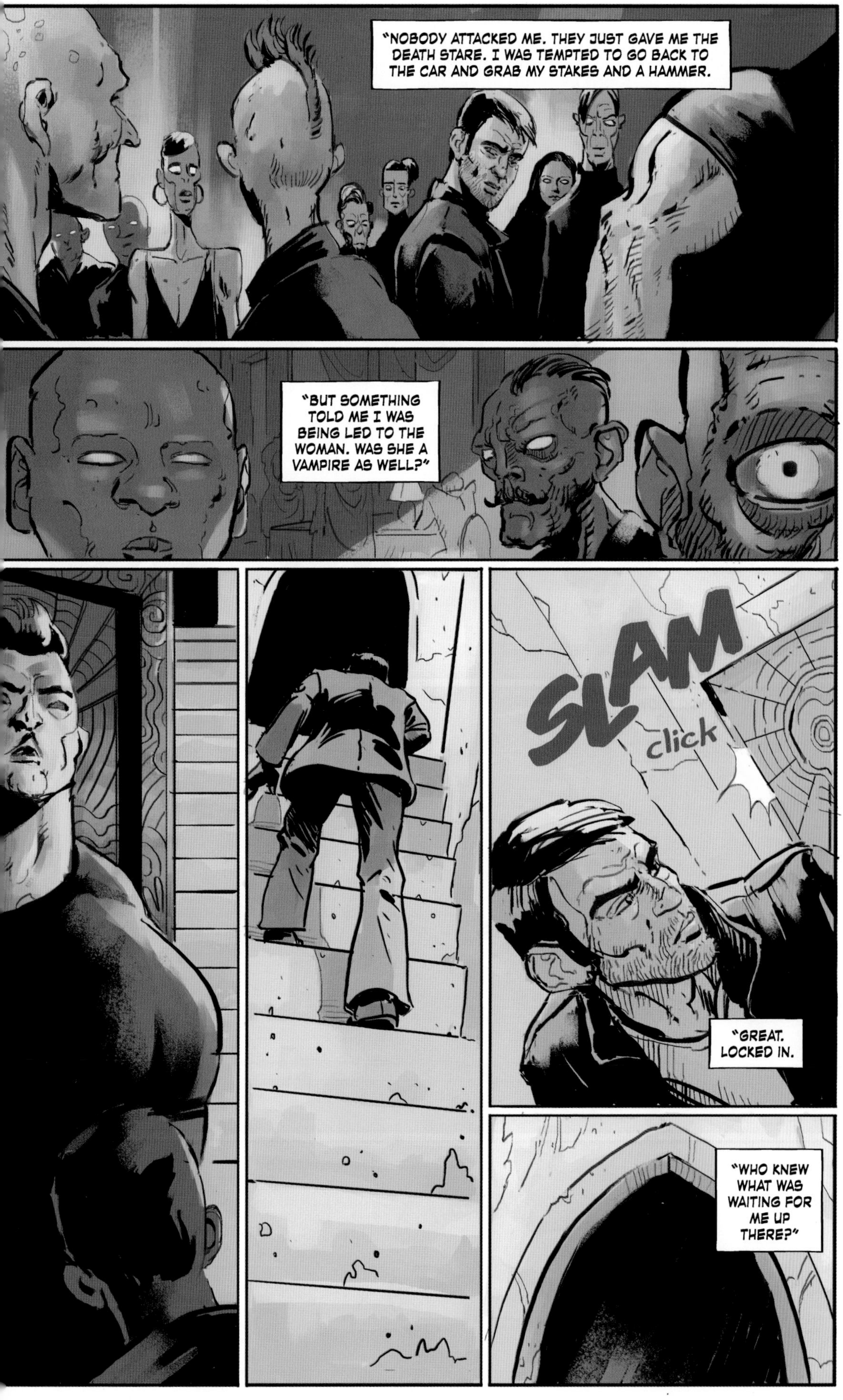
"NOBODY ATTACKED ME. THEY JUST GAVE ME THE DEATH STARE. I WAS TEMPTED TO GO BACK TO THE CAR AND GRAB MY STAKES AND A HAMMER.
"BUT SOMETHING TOLD ME I WAS BEING LED TO THE WOMAN. WAS SHE A VAMPIRE AS WELL?"
SLAM
click
"GREAT. LOCKED IN.
"WHO KNEW WHAT WAS WAITING FOR ME UP THERE?"

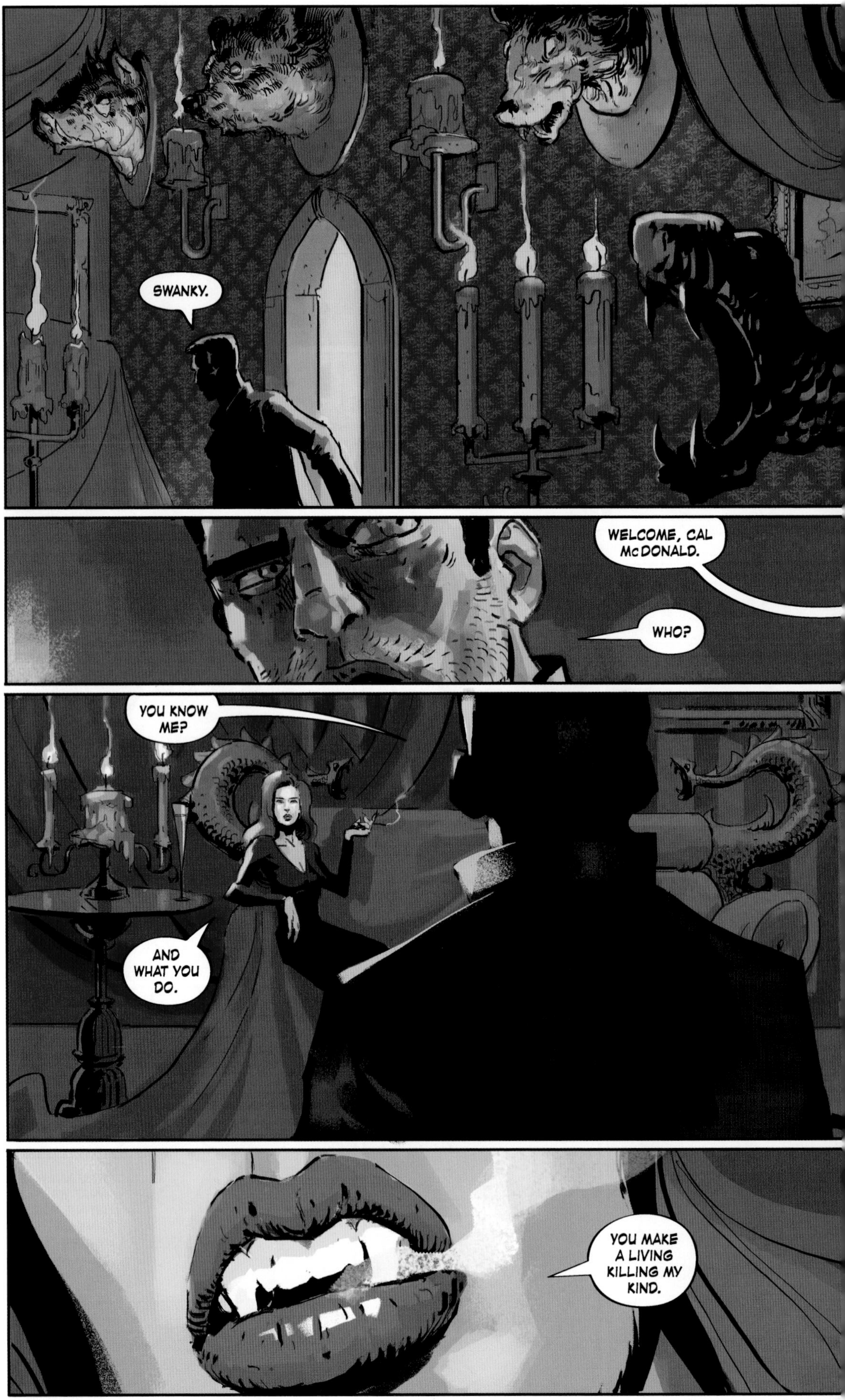
SWANKY.
WELCOME, CAL McDONALD.
WHO?
YOU KNOW ME?
AND WHAT YOU DO.
YOU MAKE A LIVING KILLING MY KIND.

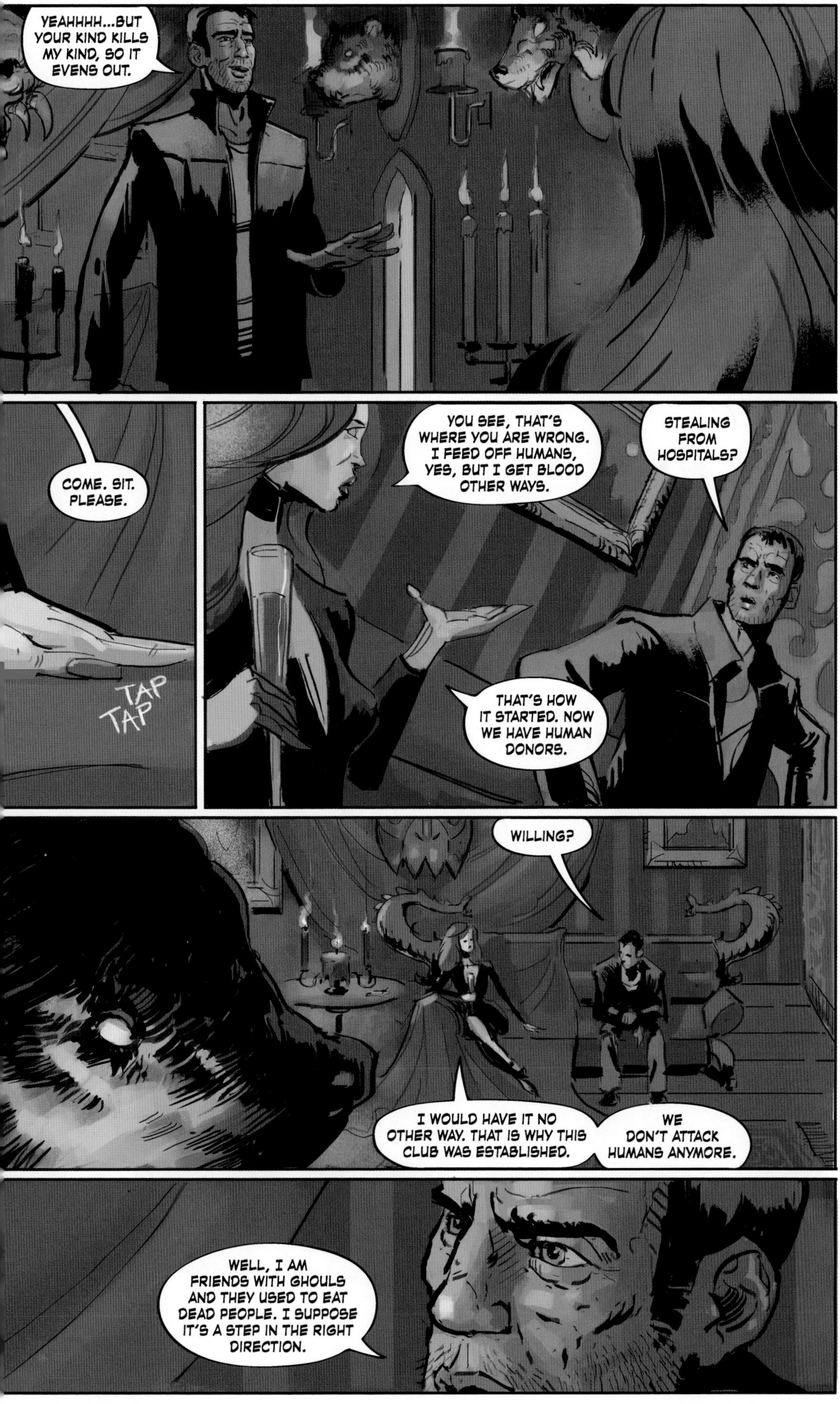
YEAHHHH...BUT YOUR KIND KILLS MY KIND, SO IT EVENS OUT.
COME. SIT. PLEASE.
TAP TAP
YOU SEE, THAT'S WHERE YOU ARE WRONG. I FEED OFF HUMANS, YES, BUT I GET BLOOD OTHER WAYS.
STEALING FROM HOSPITALS?
THAT'S HOW IT STARTED. NOW WE HAVE HUMAN DONORS.
WILLING?
I WOULD HAVE IT NO OTHER WAY. THAT IS WHY THIS CLUB WAS ESTABLISHED.
WE DON'T ATTACK HUMANS ANYMORE.
WELL, I AM FRIENDS WITH GHOULS AND THEY USED TO EAT DEAD PEOPLE. I SUPPOSE IT'S A STEP IN THE RIGHT DIRECTION.

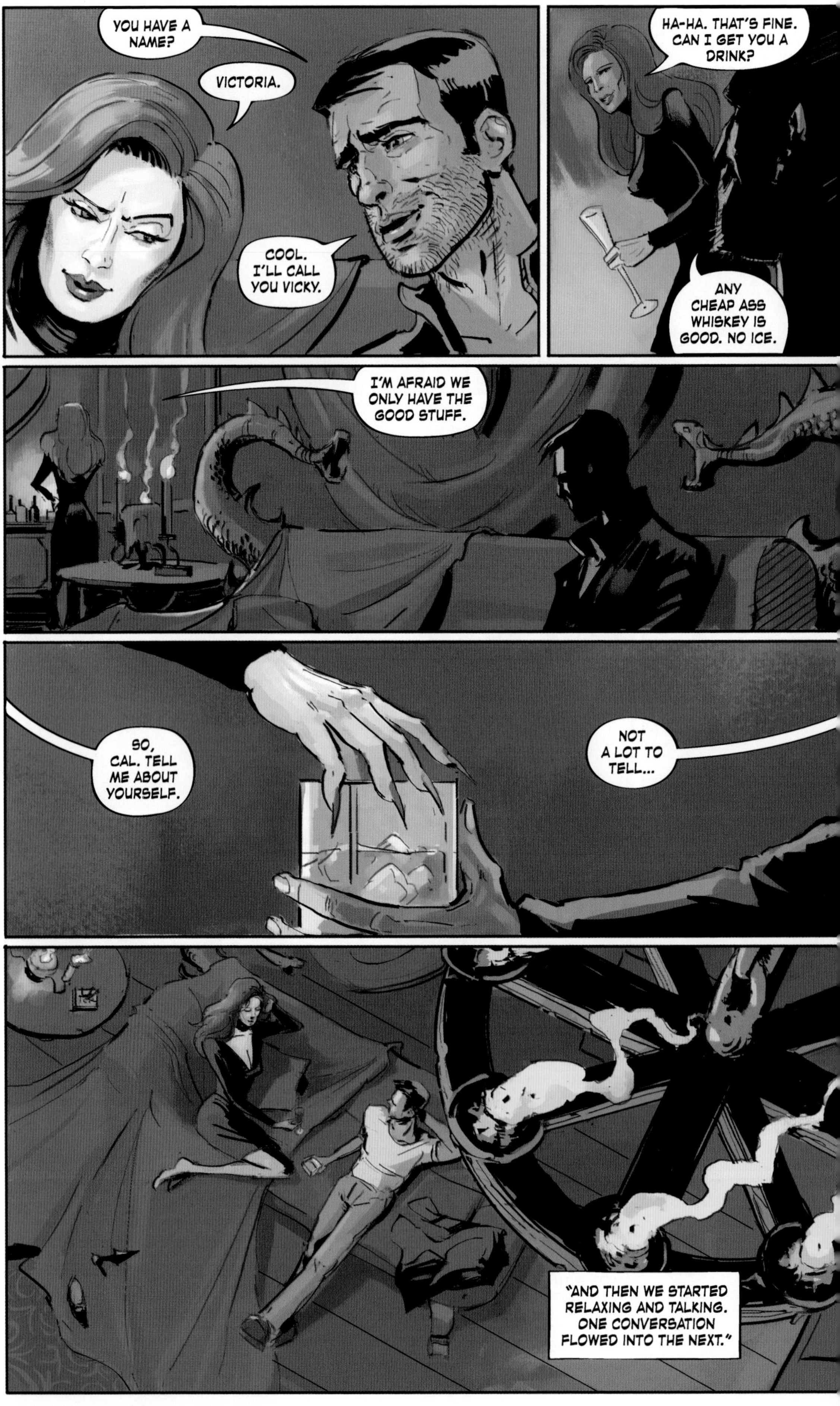
YOU HAVE A NAME?
VICTORIA.
COOL. I'LL CALL YOU VICKY.
HA-HA. THAT'S FINE. CAN I GET YOU A DRINK?
ANY CHEAP ASS WHISKEY IS GOOD. NO ICE.
I'M AFRAID WE ONLY HAVE THE GOOD STUFF.
SO, CAL. TELL ME ABOUT YOURSELF.
NOT A LOT TO TELL...
"AND THEN WE STARTED RELAXING AND TALKING. ONE CONVERSATION FLOWED INTO THE NEXT."

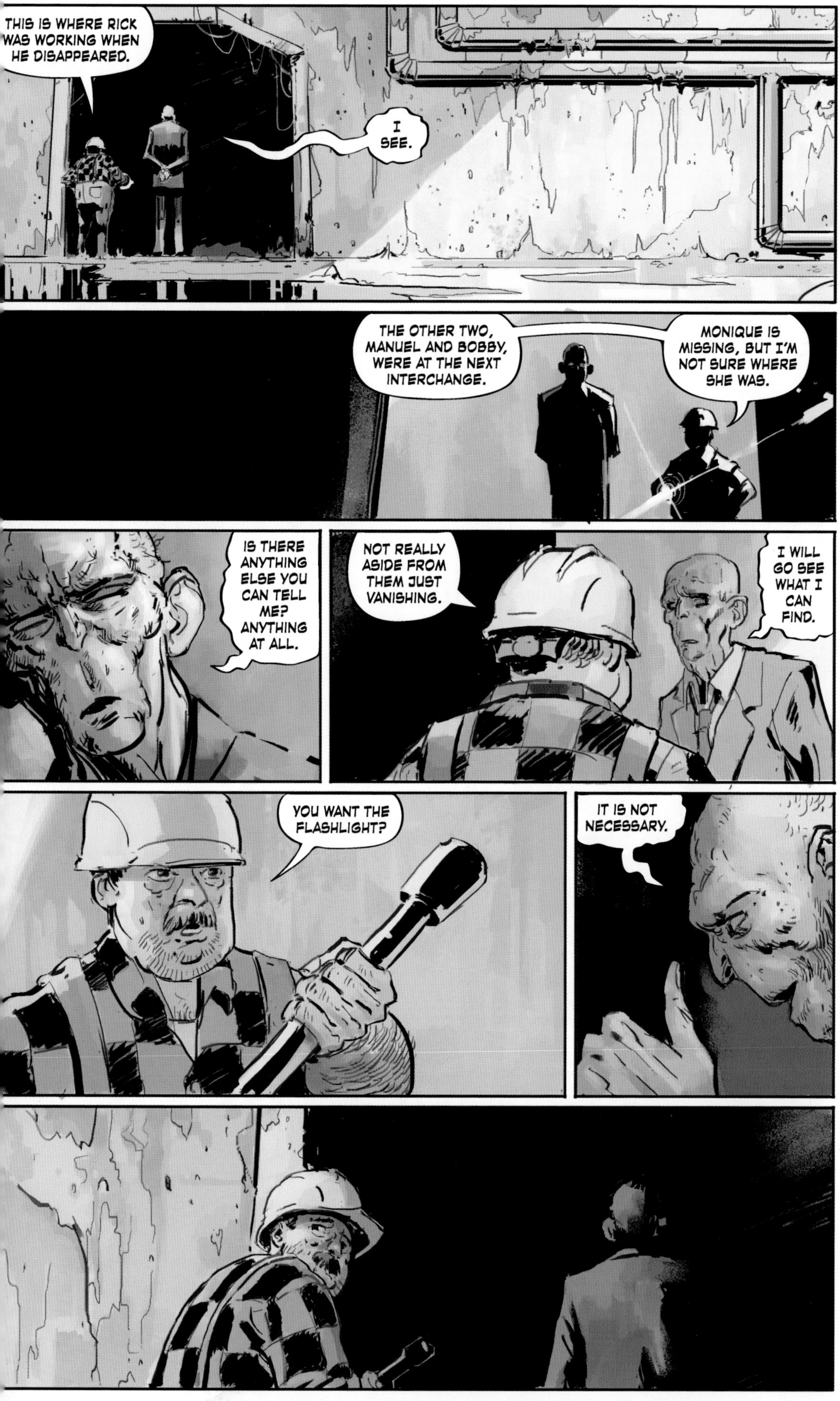
THIS IS WHERE RICK WAS WORKING WHEN HE DISAPPEARED.
I SEE.
THE OTHER TWO, MANUEL AND BOBBY, WERE AT THE NEXT INTERCHANGE.
MONIQUE IS MISSING, BUT I'M NOT SURE WHERE SHE WAS.
IS THERE ANYTHING ELSE YOU CAN TELL ME? ANYTHING AT ALL.
NOT REALLY ASIDE FROM THEM JUST VANISHING.
I WILL GO SEE WHAT I CAN FIND.
YOU WANT THE FLASHLIGHT?
IT IS NOT NECESSARY.

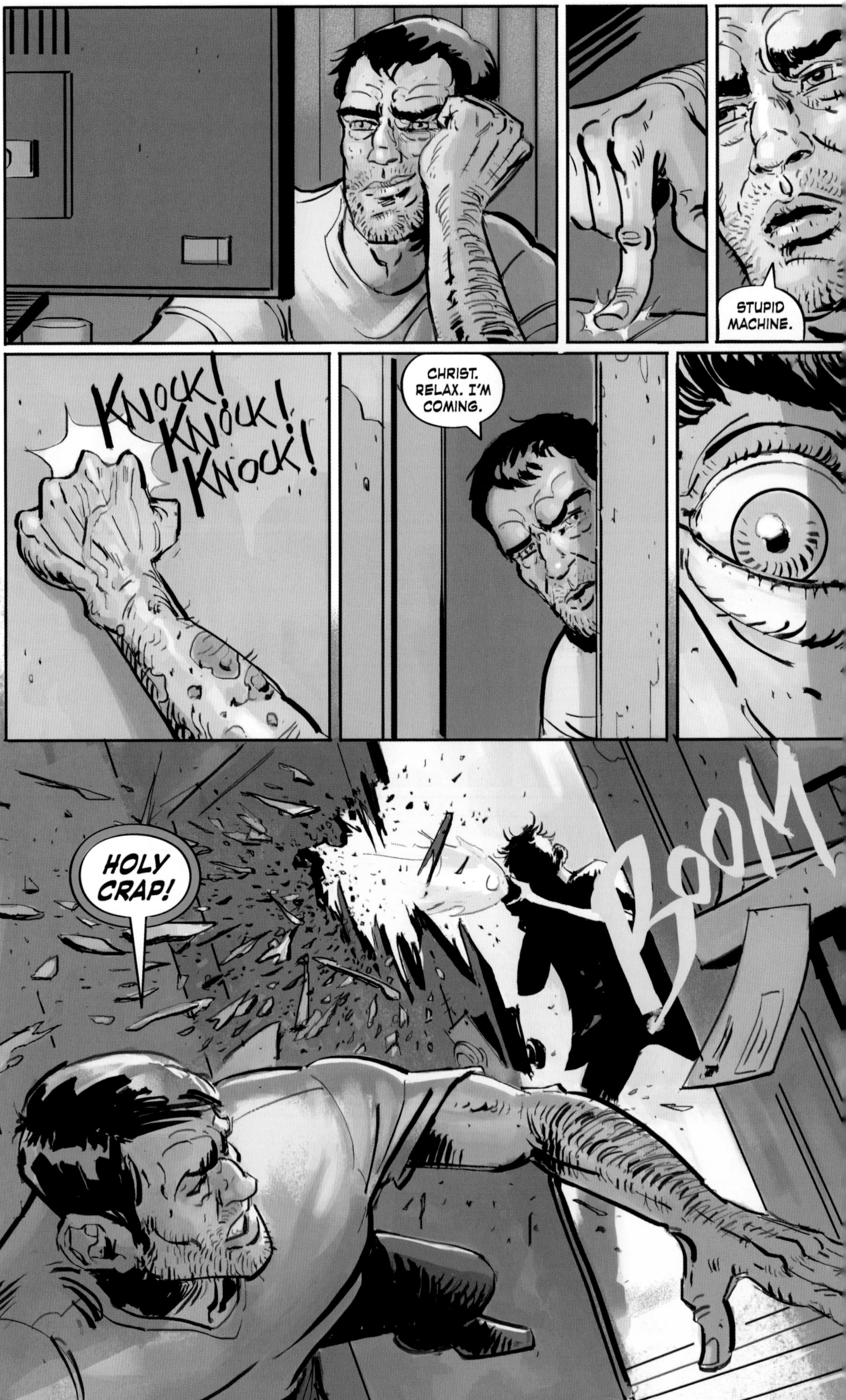
STUPID MACHINE.
KNOCK! KNOCK! KNOCK!
CHRIST. RELAX. I'M COMING.
HOLY CRAP!
BOOM

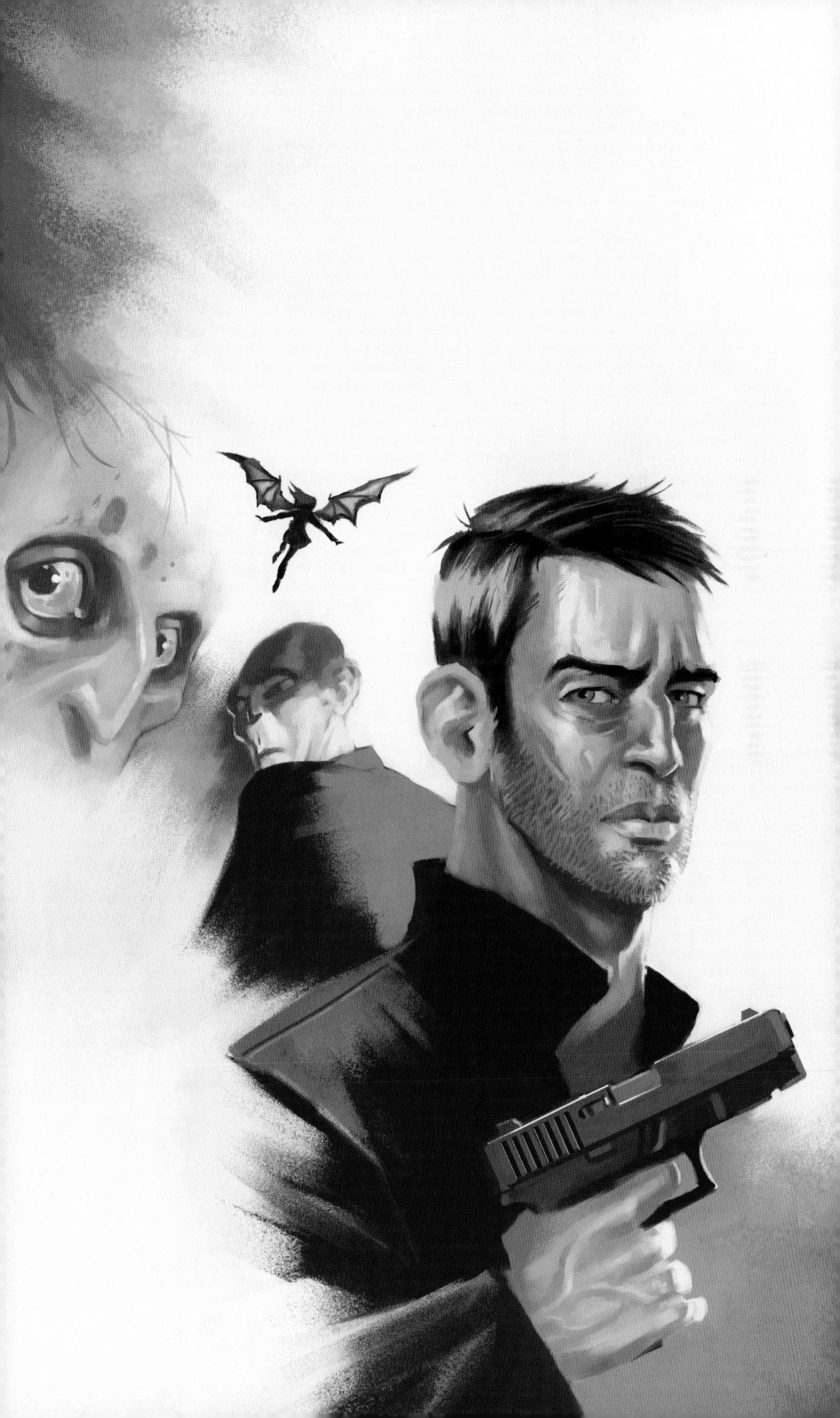

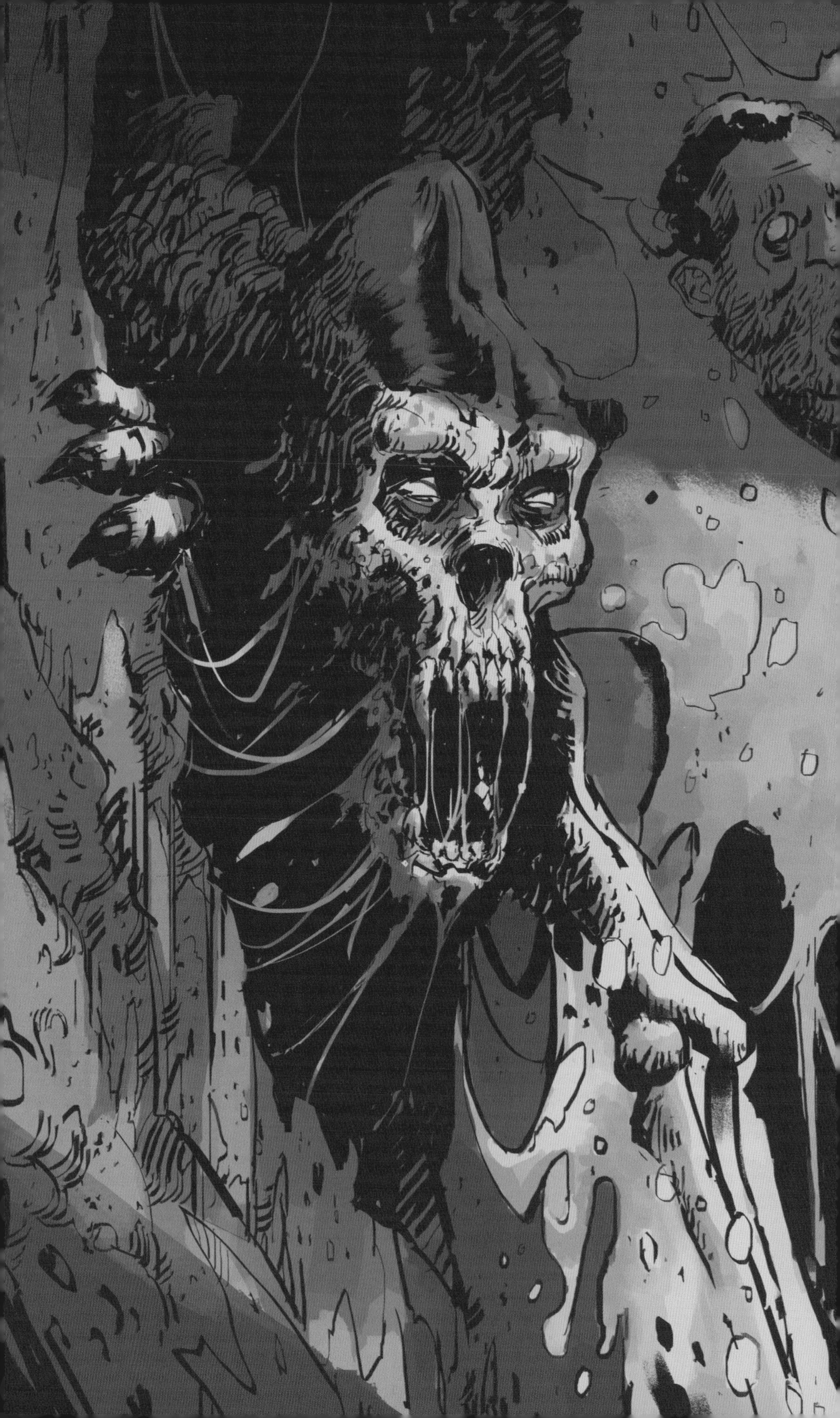

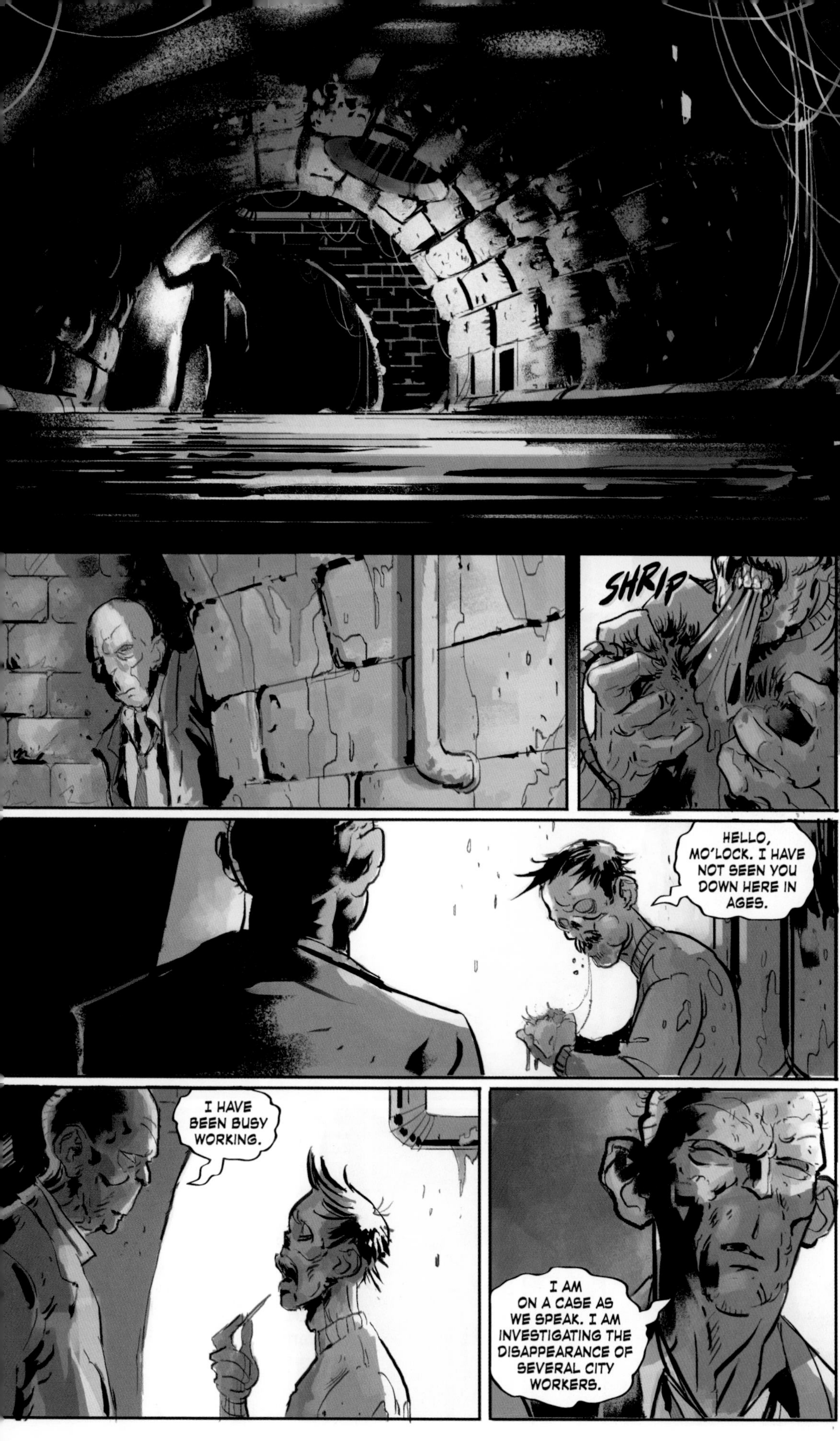
SHRIP
HELLO, MO'LOCK. I HAVE NOT SEEN YOU DOWN HERE IN AGES.
I HAVE BEEN BUSY WORKING.
I AM ON A CASE AS WE SPEAK. I AM INVESTIGATING THE DISAPPEARANCE OF SEVERAL CITY WORKERS.

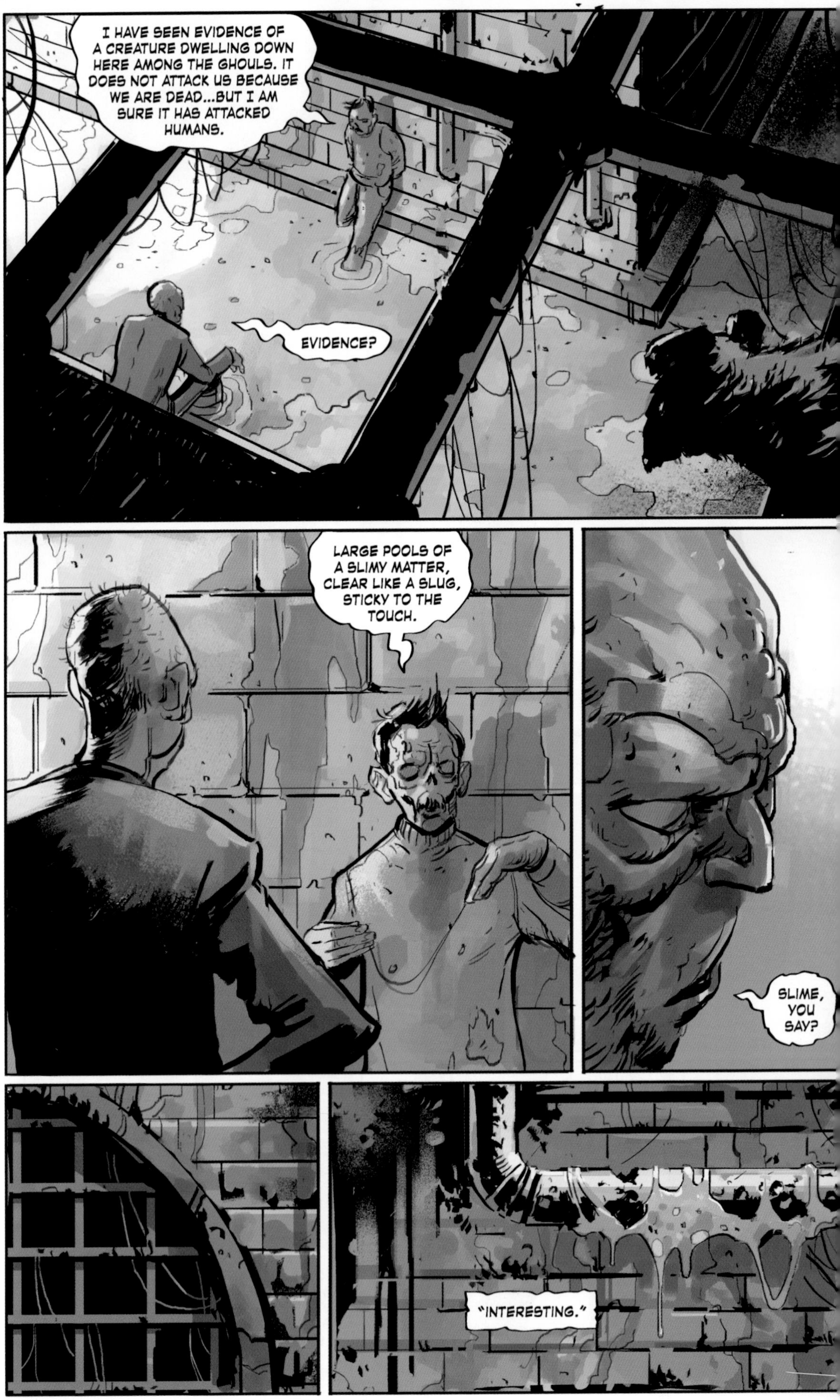
I HAVE SEEN EVIDENCE OF A CREATURE DWELLING DOWN HERE AMONG THE GHOULS. IT DOES NOT ATTACK US BECAUSE WE ARE DEAD...BUT I AM SURE IT HAS ATTACKED HUMANS.
EVIDENCE?
LARGE POOLS OF A SLIMY MATTER, CLEAR LIKE A SLUG, STICKY TO THE TOUCH.
SLIME, YOU SAY?
"INTERESTING."

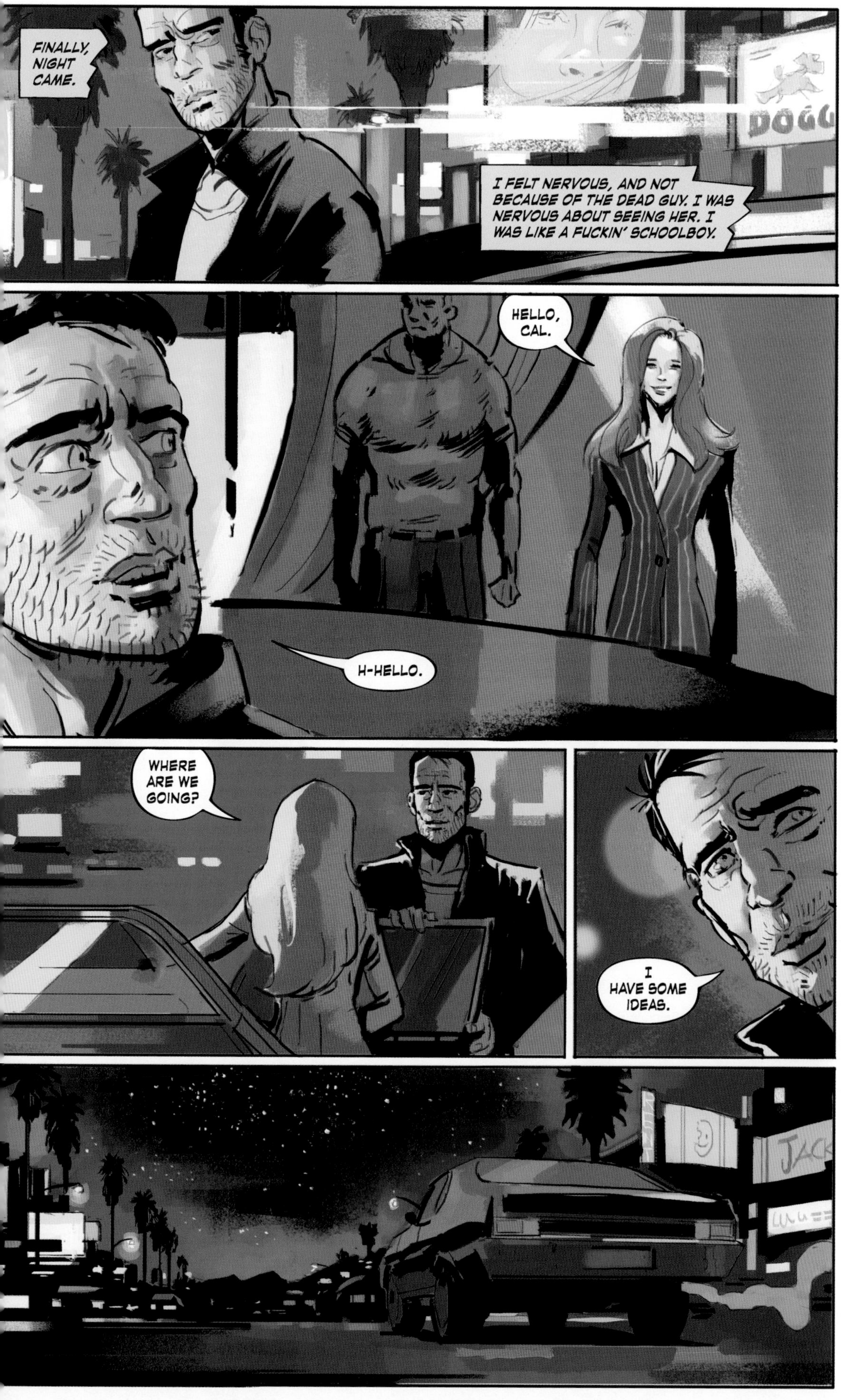
FINALLY, NIGHT CAME.
I FELT NERVOUS, AND NOT BECAUSE OF THE DEAD GUY. I WAS NERVOUS ABOUT SEEING HER. I WAS LIKE A FUCKIN' SCHOOLBOY.
HELLO, CAL.
H-HELLO.
WHERE ARE WE GOING?
I HAVE SOME IDEAS.

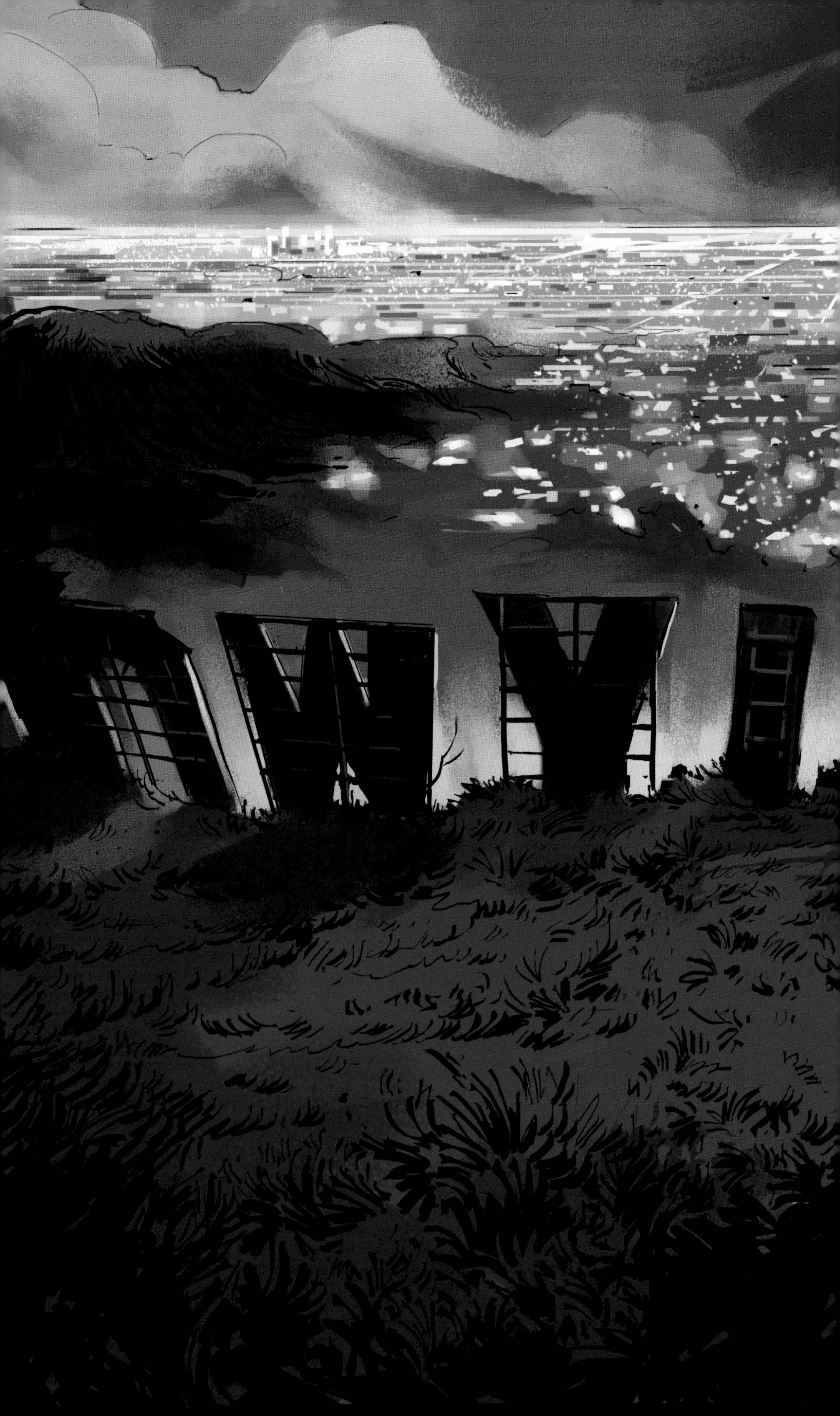

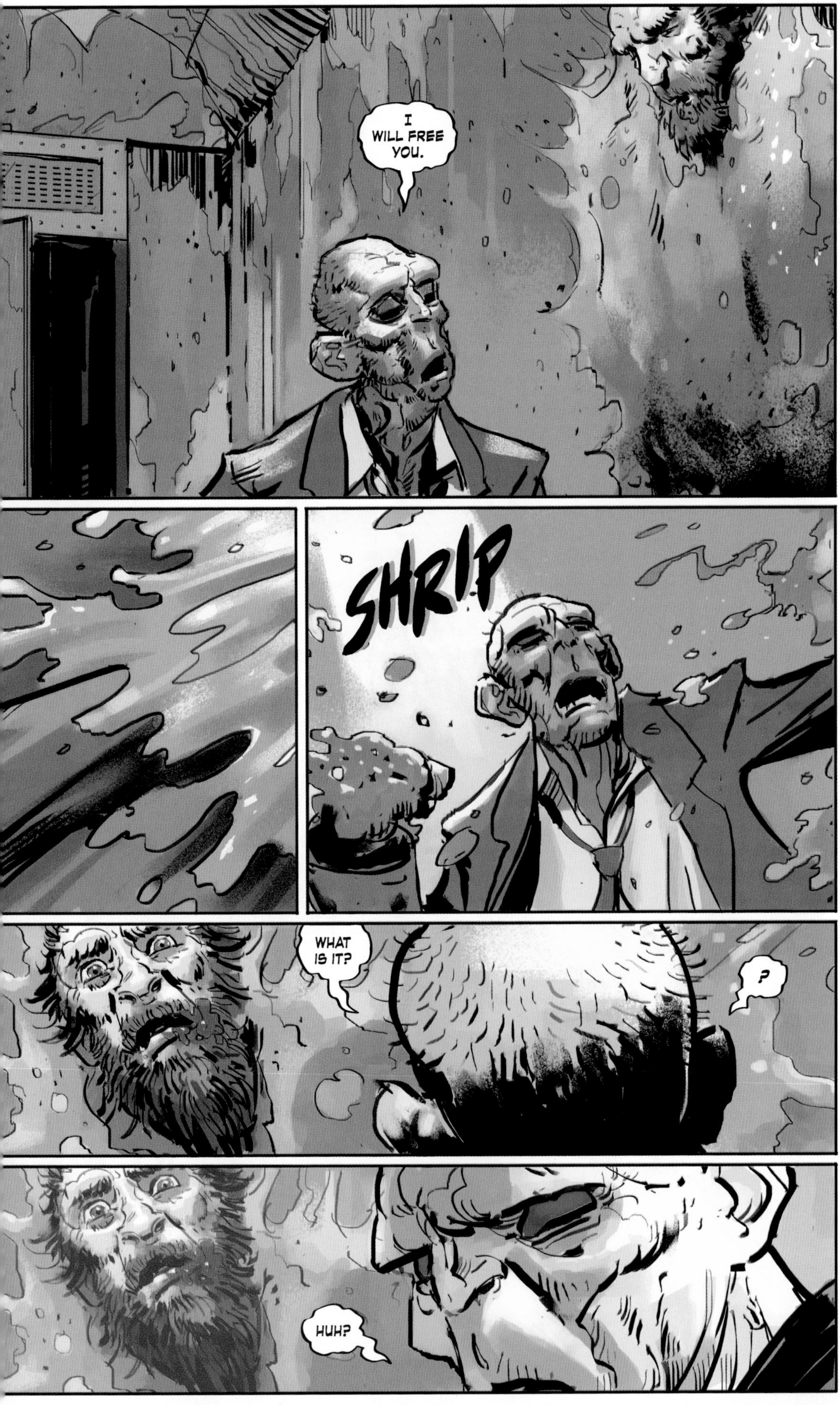
I WILL FREE YOU.
SHRIP
WHAT IS IT?
?
HUH?

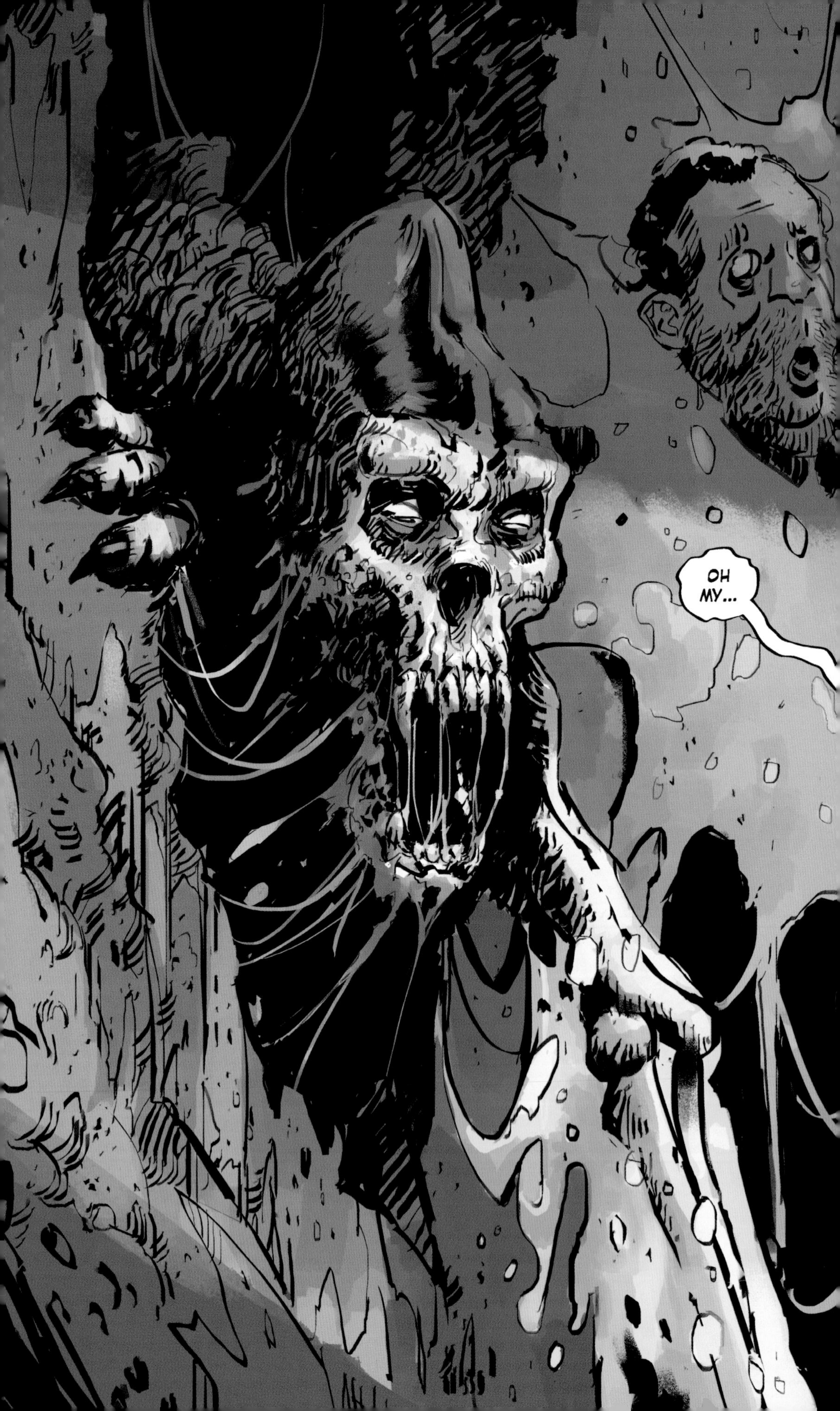
OH MY...

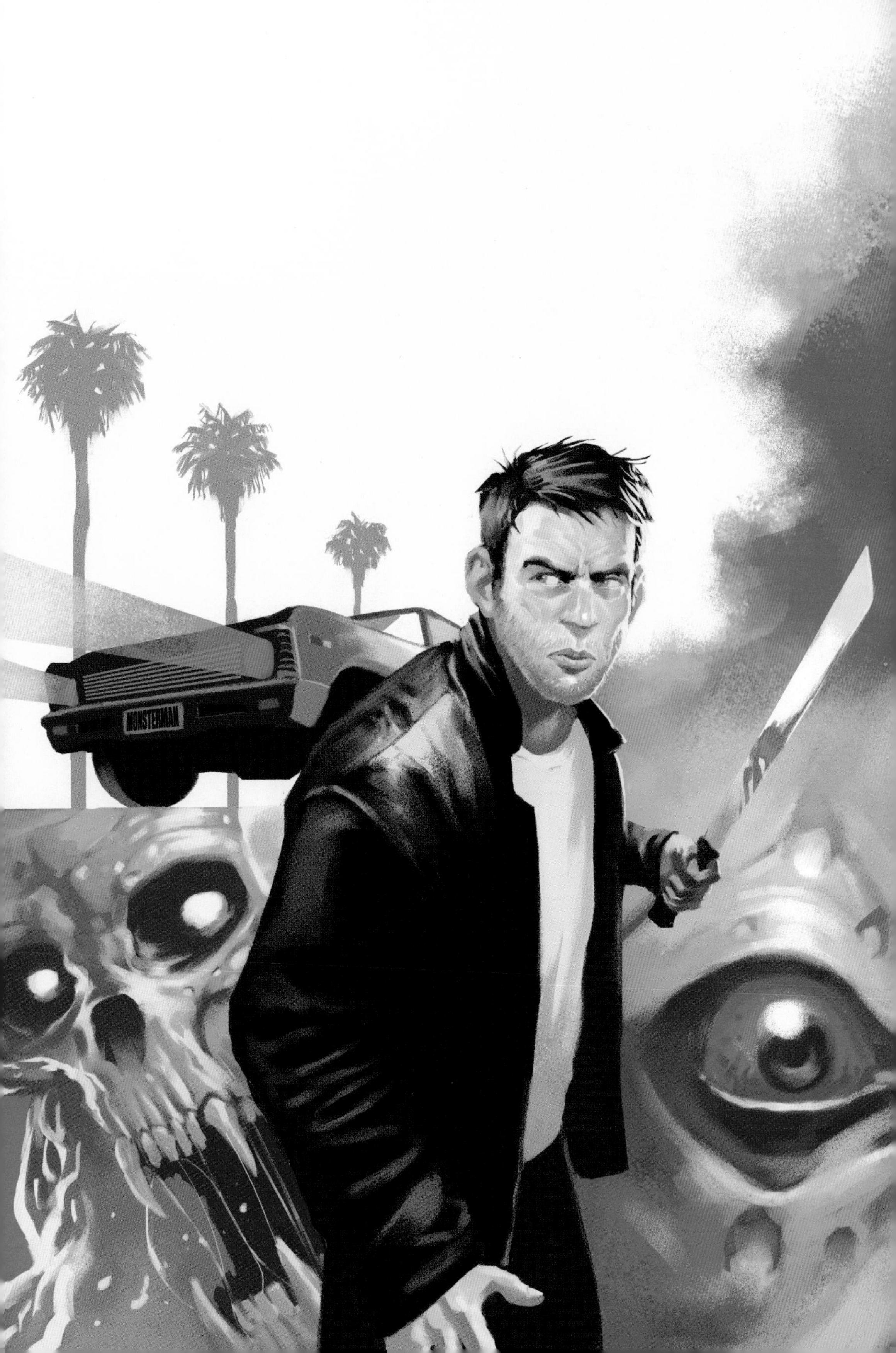
MONSTERMAN

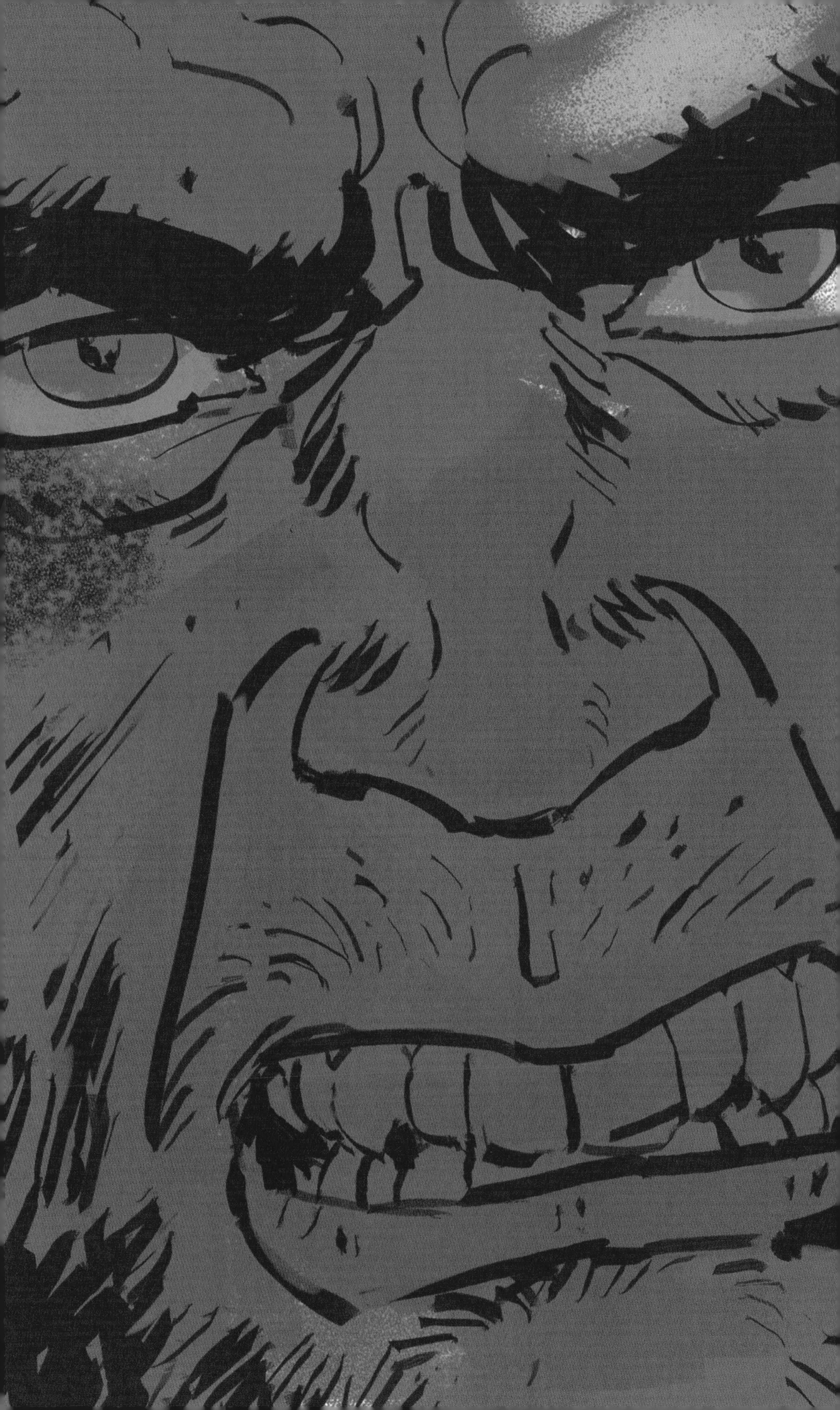

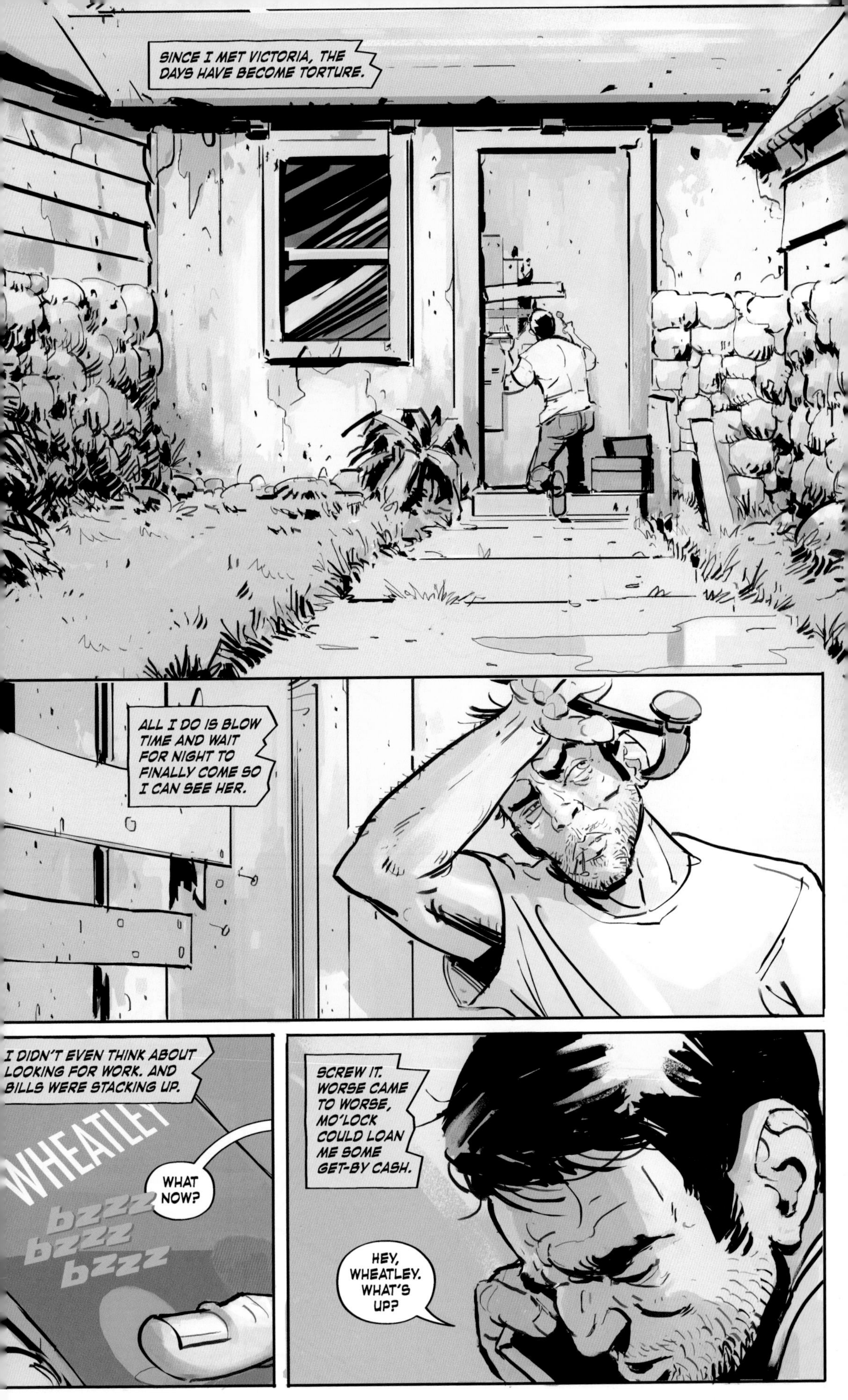
SINCE I MET VICTORIA, THE DAYS HAVE BECOME TORTURE.
ALL I DO IS BLOW TIME AND WAIT FOR NIGHT TO FINALLY COME SO I CAN SEE HER.
I DIDN'T EVEN THINK ABOUT LOOKING FOR WORK. AND BILLS WERE STACKING UP.
WHEATLEY
bzzz bzzz bzzz
WHAT NOW?
SCREW IT. WORSE CAME TO WORSE, MO'LOCK COULD LOAN ME SOME GET-BY CASH.
HEY, WHEATLEY. WHAT'S UP?

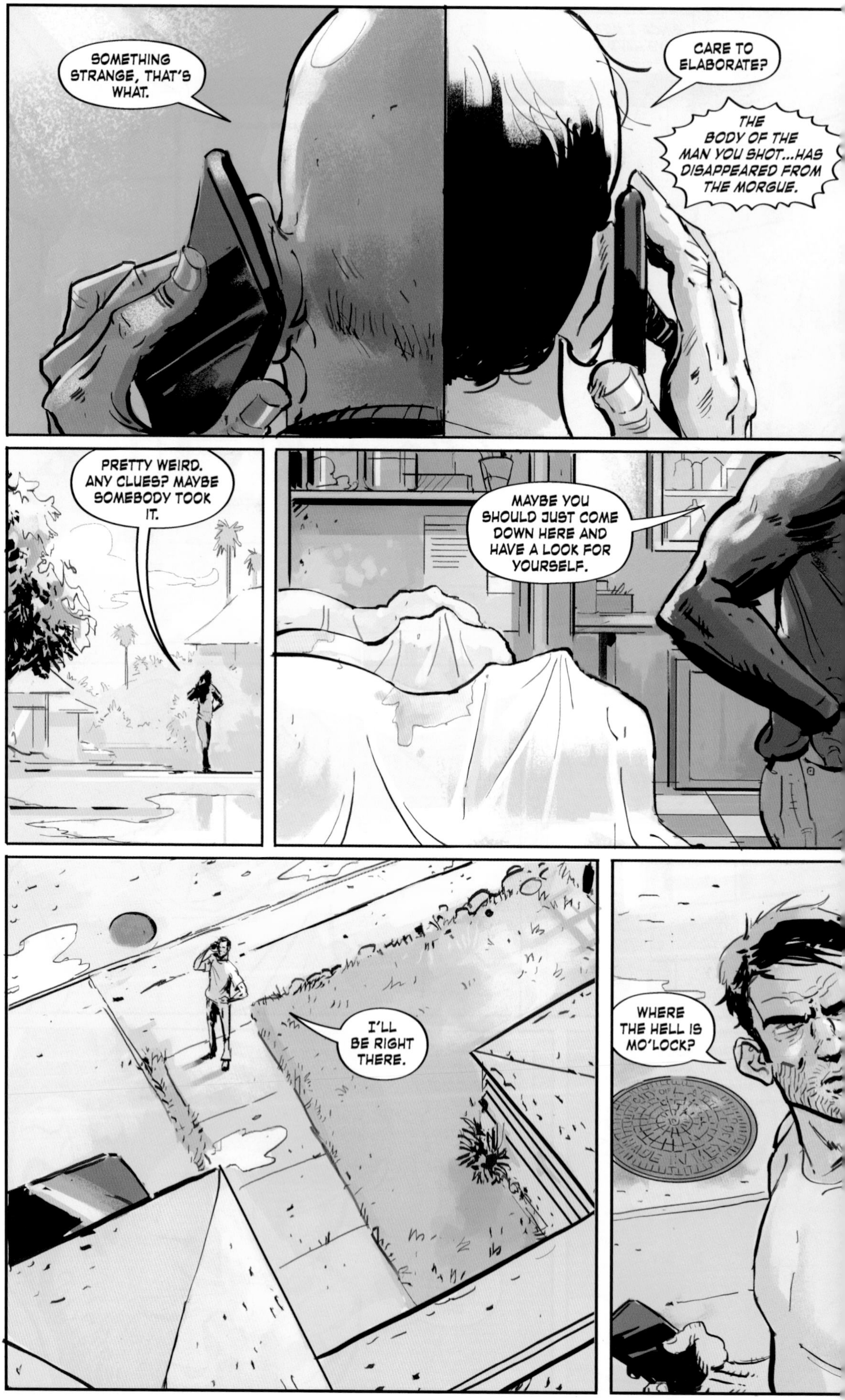

SOMETHING STRANGE, THAT'S WHAT.
CARE TO ELABORATE?
THE BODY OF THE MAN YOU SHOT...HAS DISAPPEARED FROM THE MORGUE.
PRETTY WEIRD. ANY CLUES? MAYBE SOMEBODY TOOK IT.
MAYBE YOU SHOULD JUST COME DOWN HERE AND HAVE A LOOK FOR YOURSELF.
I'LL BE RIGHT THERE.
WHERE THE HELL IS MO'LOCK?

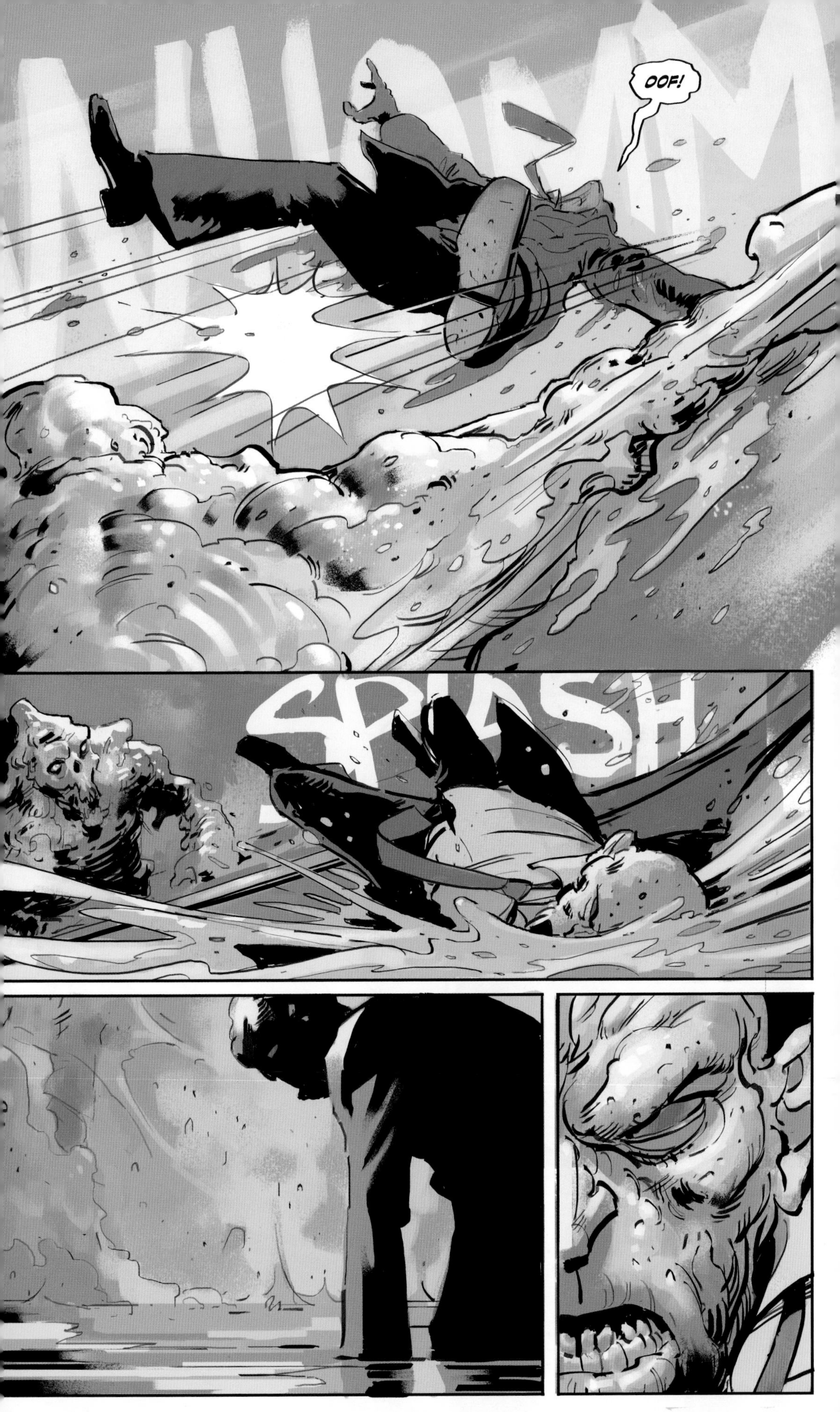
OOF!

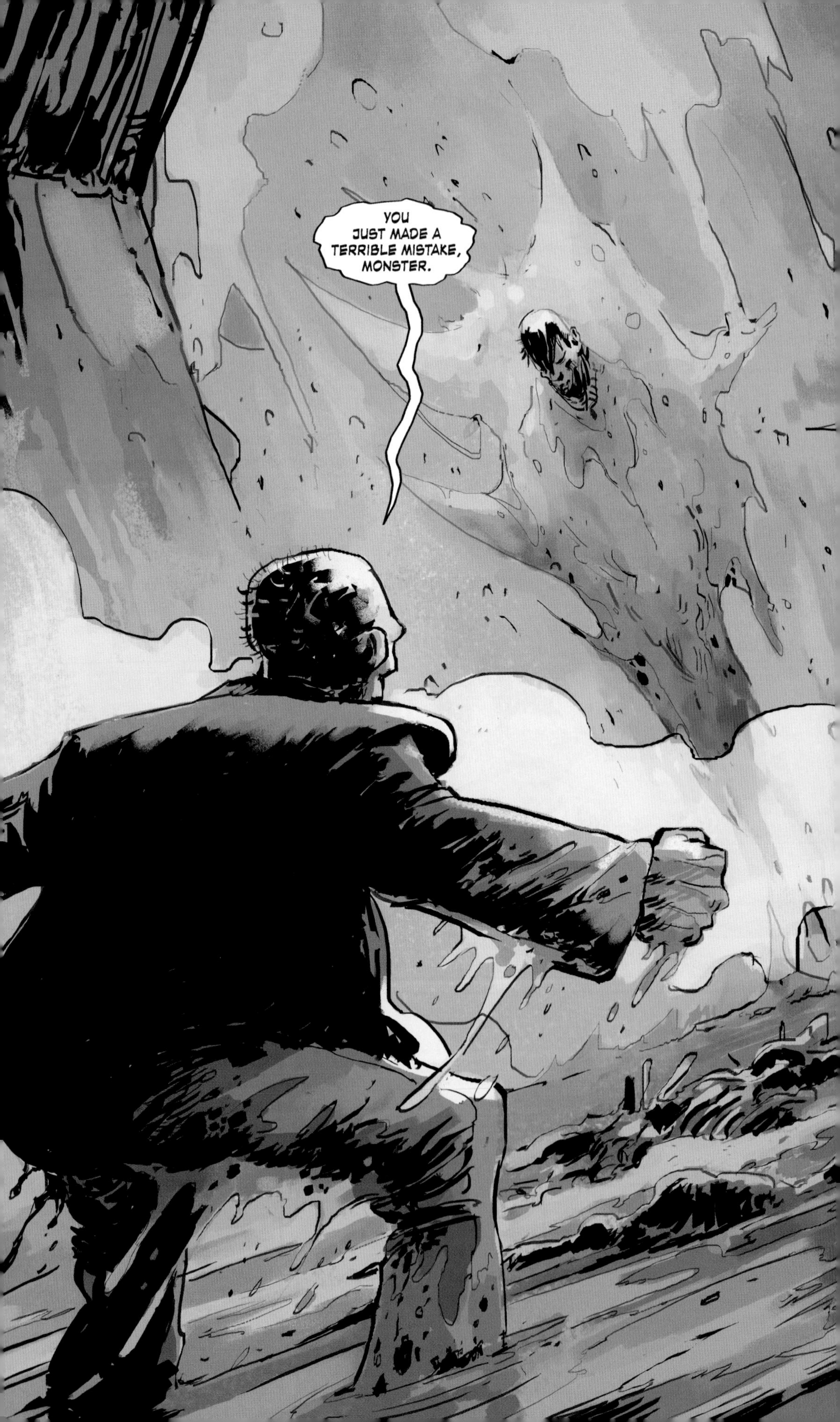
YOU JUST MADE A TERRIBLE MISTAKE, MONSTER.

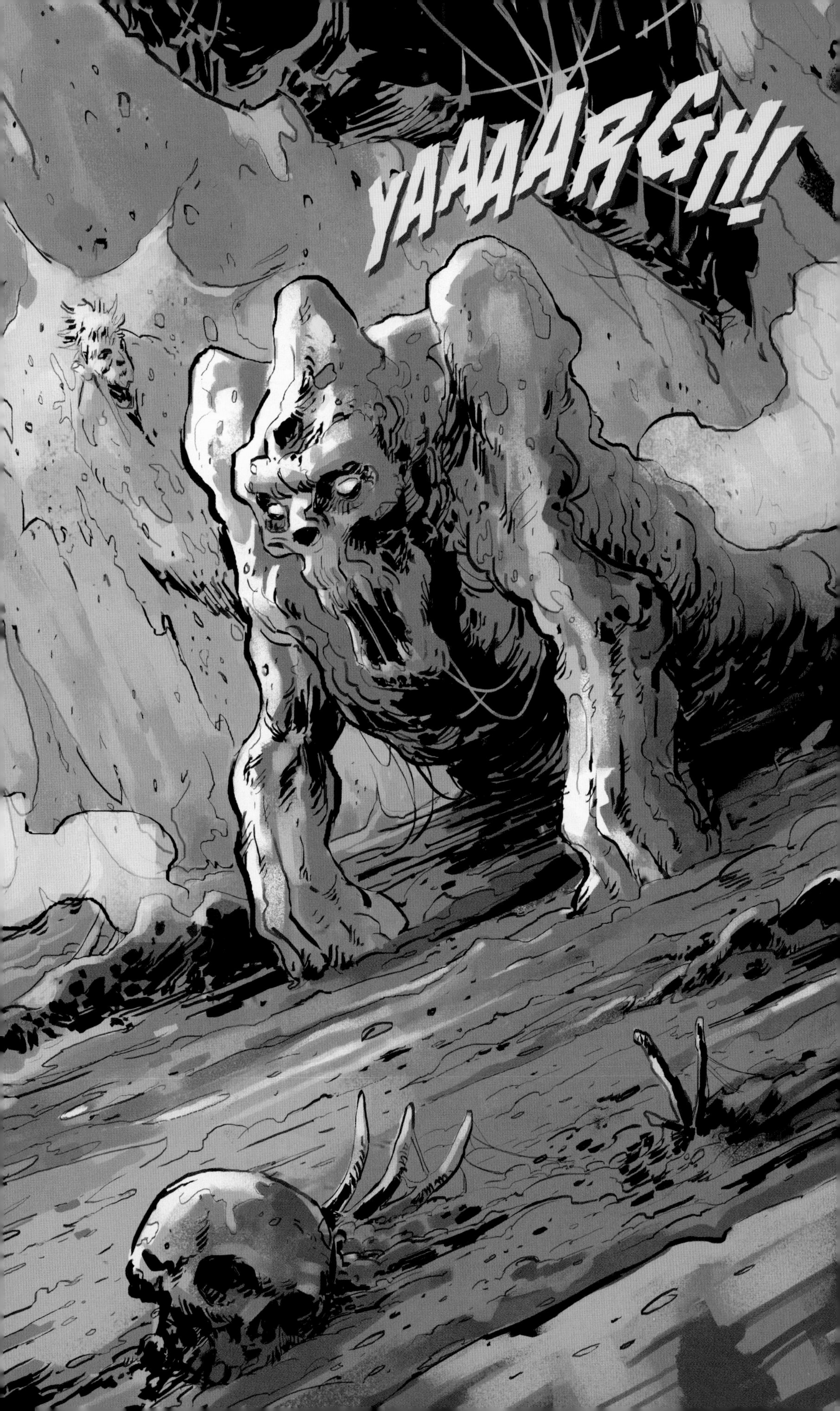
YAAAARGH!

SWOOP

SPLAK

ALL I HAD TO DO WAS GO HOME AND WAIT.

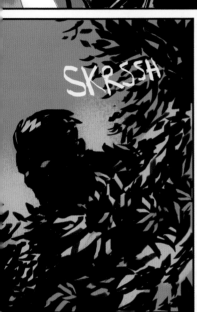

SKRSSH

TRYING TO SNEAK UP ON ME, EH?

DON'T SHOOT...

THE DOORMAN?!

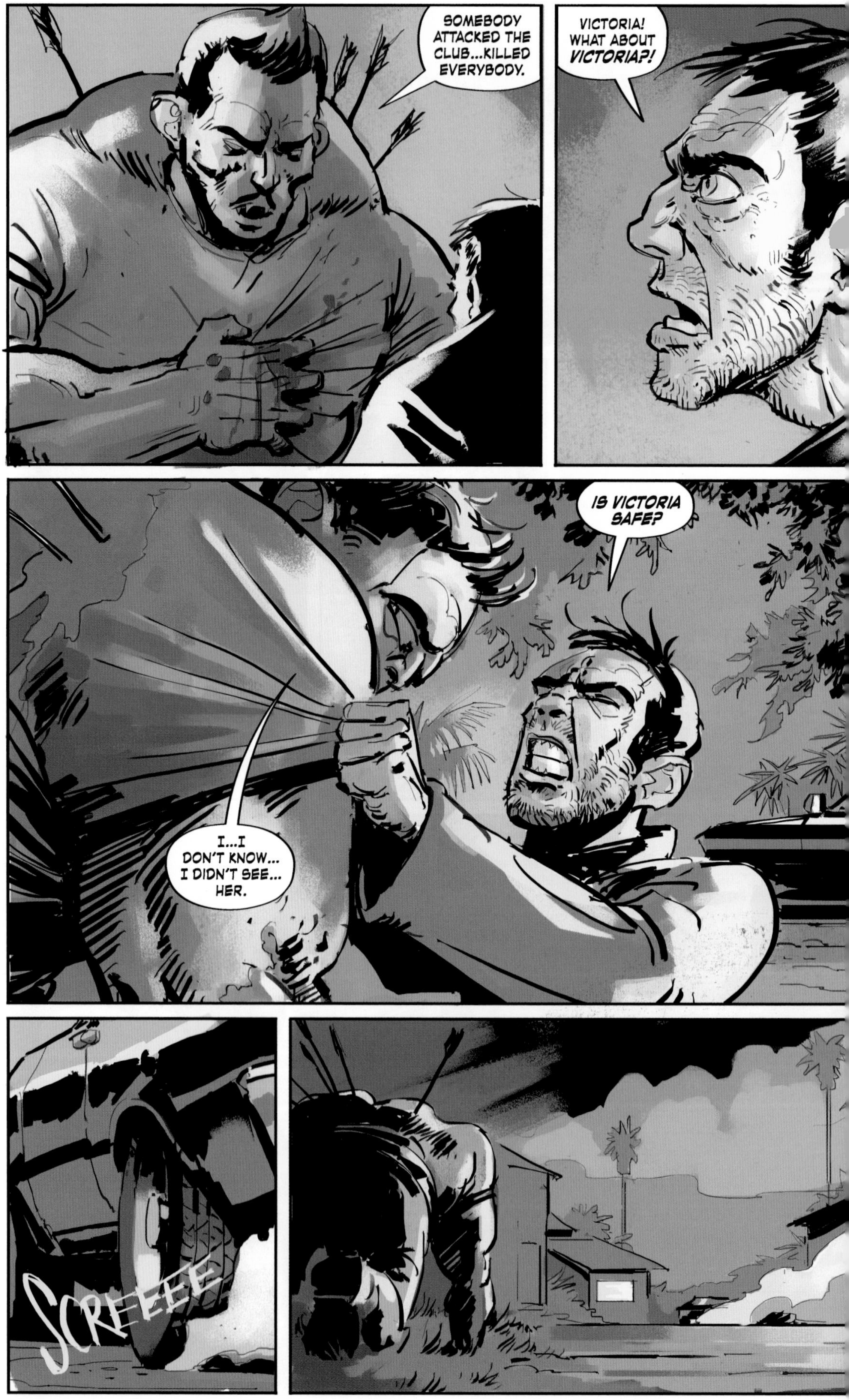
SOMEBODY ATTACKED THE CLUB...KILLED EVERYBODY.
VICTORIA! WHAT ABOUT *VICTORIA?!*
IS VICTORIA SAFE?
I...I DON'T KNOW... I DIDN'T SEE... HER.
SCREEEE

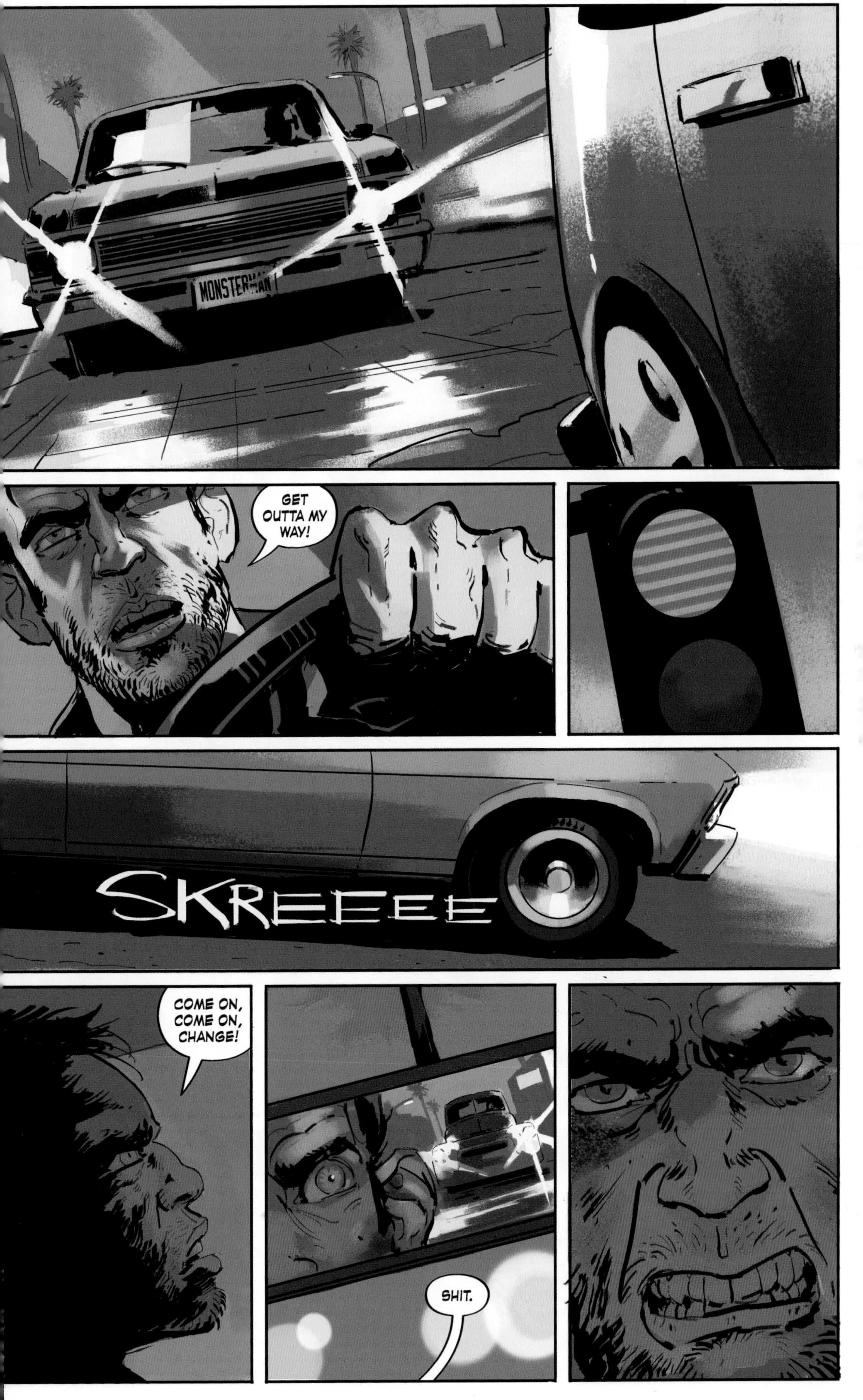
MONSTERMAN
GET OUTTA MY WAY!
SKREEEE
COME ON, COME ON, CHANGE!
SHIT.

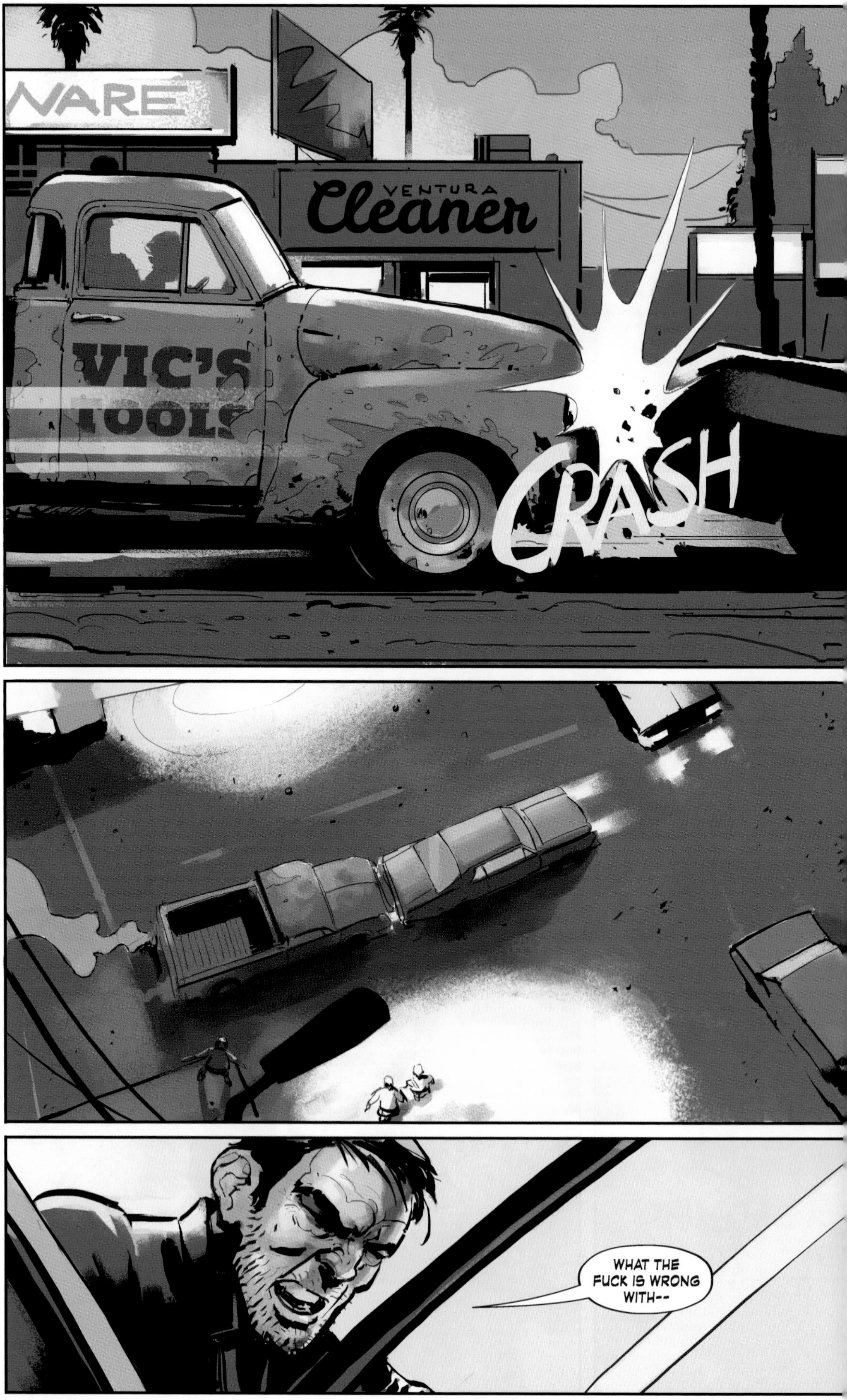
NARE
VENTURA
Cleaner
VIC'S
TOOLS
CRASH
WHAT THE FUCK IS WRONG WITH--

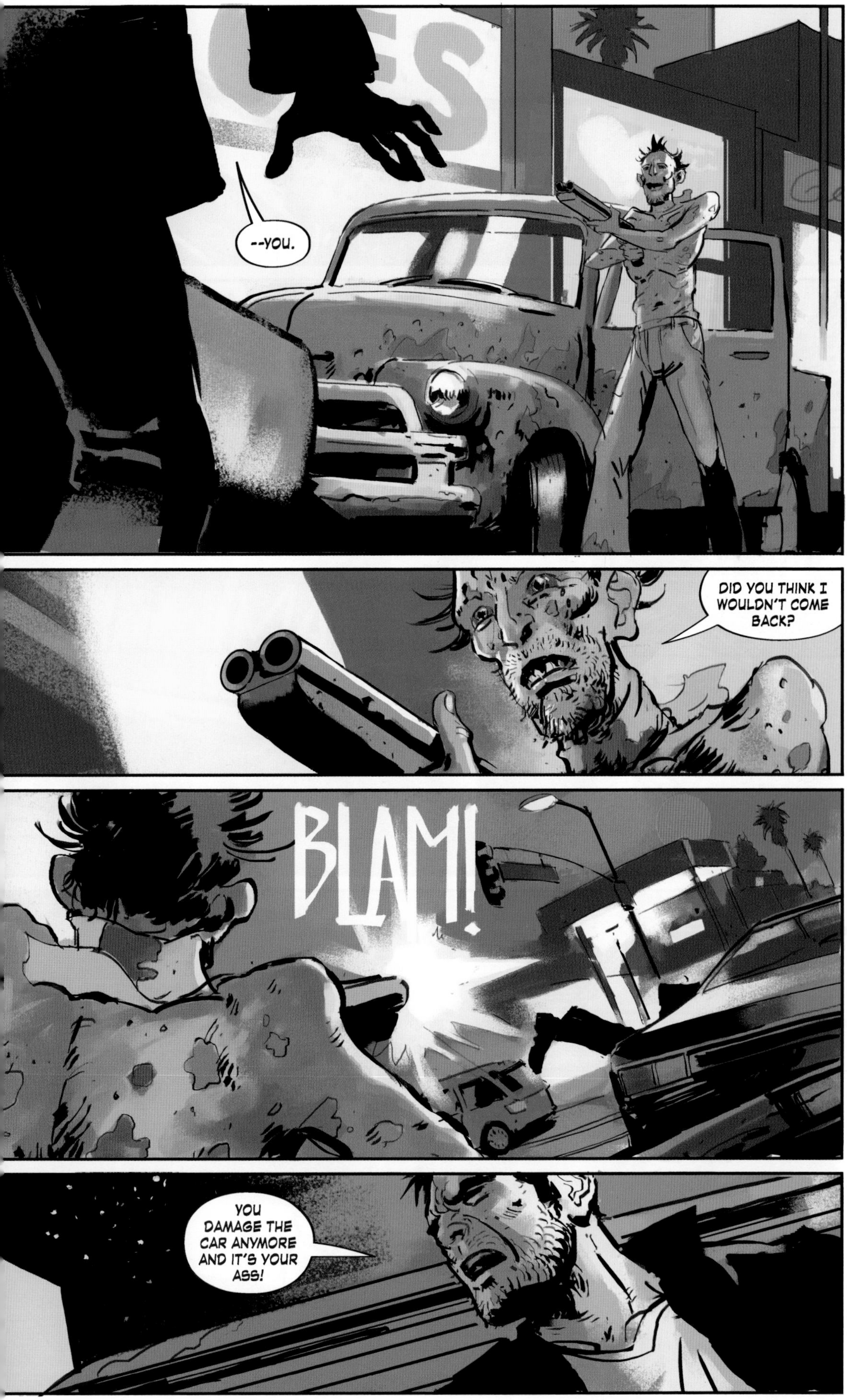
--YOU.
DID YOU THINK I WOULDN'T COME BACK?
BLAM!
YOU DAMAGE THE CAR ANYMORE AND IT'S YOUR ASS!

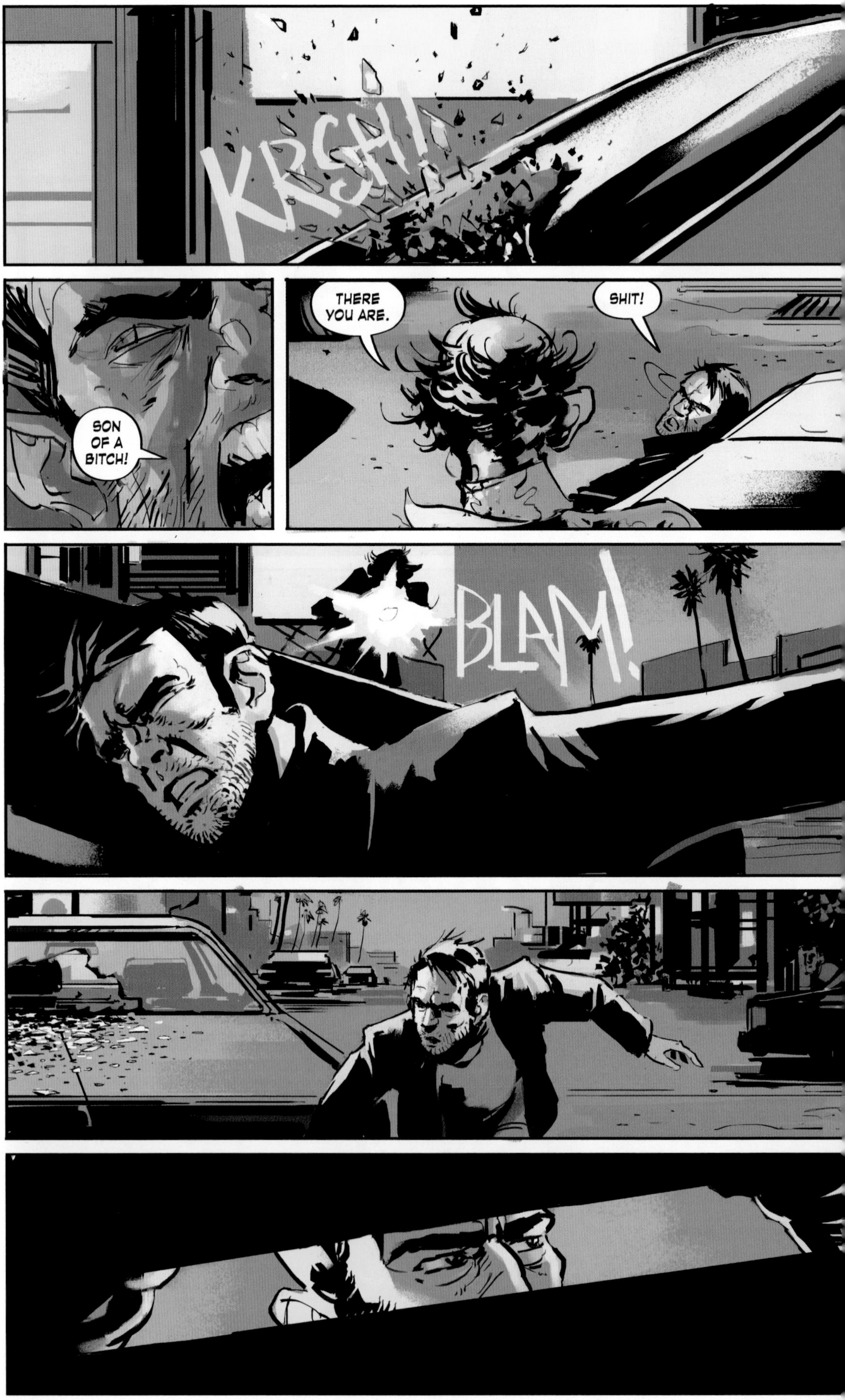
KRGH!
SON OF A BITCH!
THERE YOU ARE.
SHIT!
BLAM!

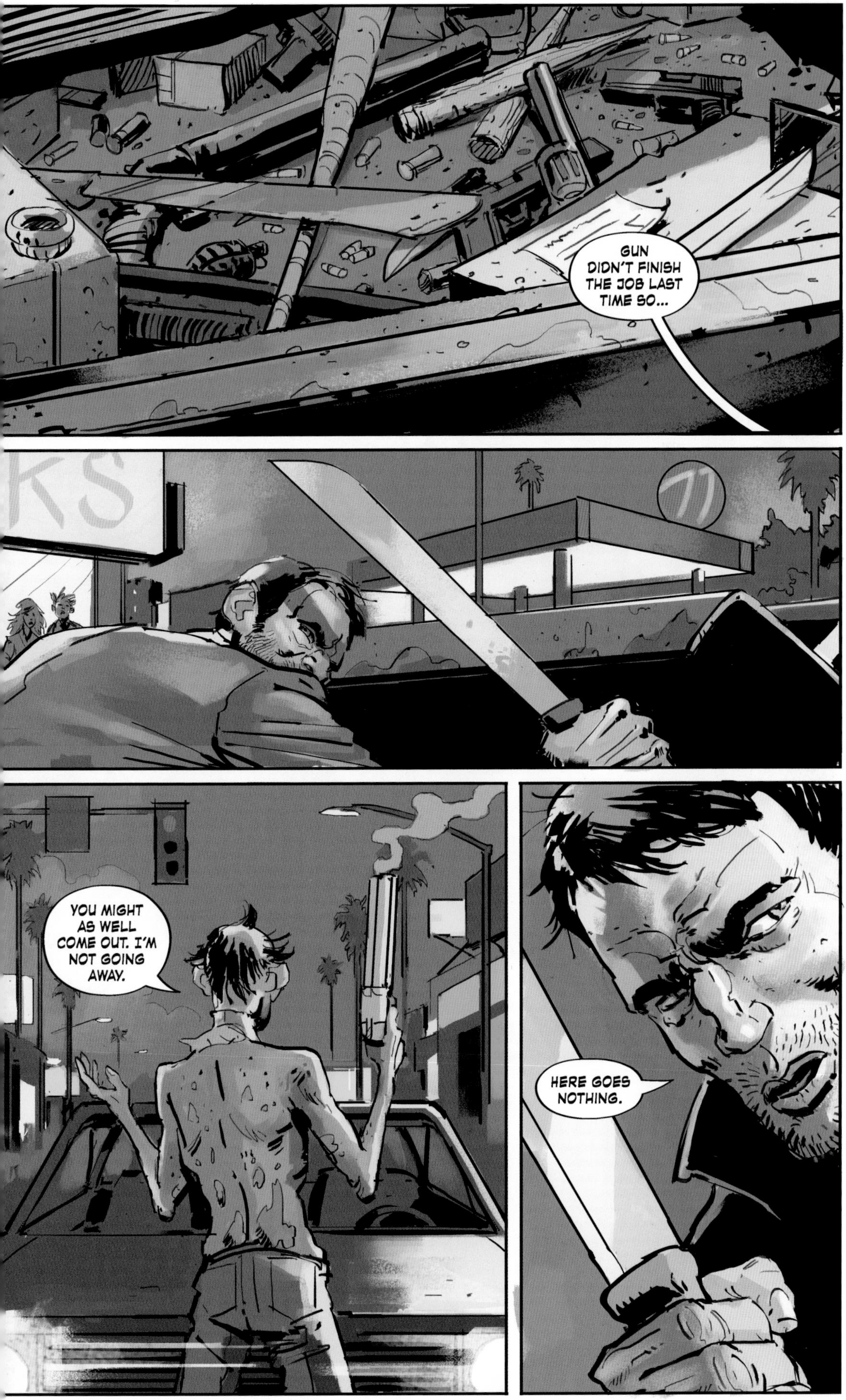
GUN DIDN'T FINISH THE JOB LAST TIME SO...
YOU MIGHT AS WELL COME OUT. I'M NOT GOING AWAY.
HERE GOES NOTHING.

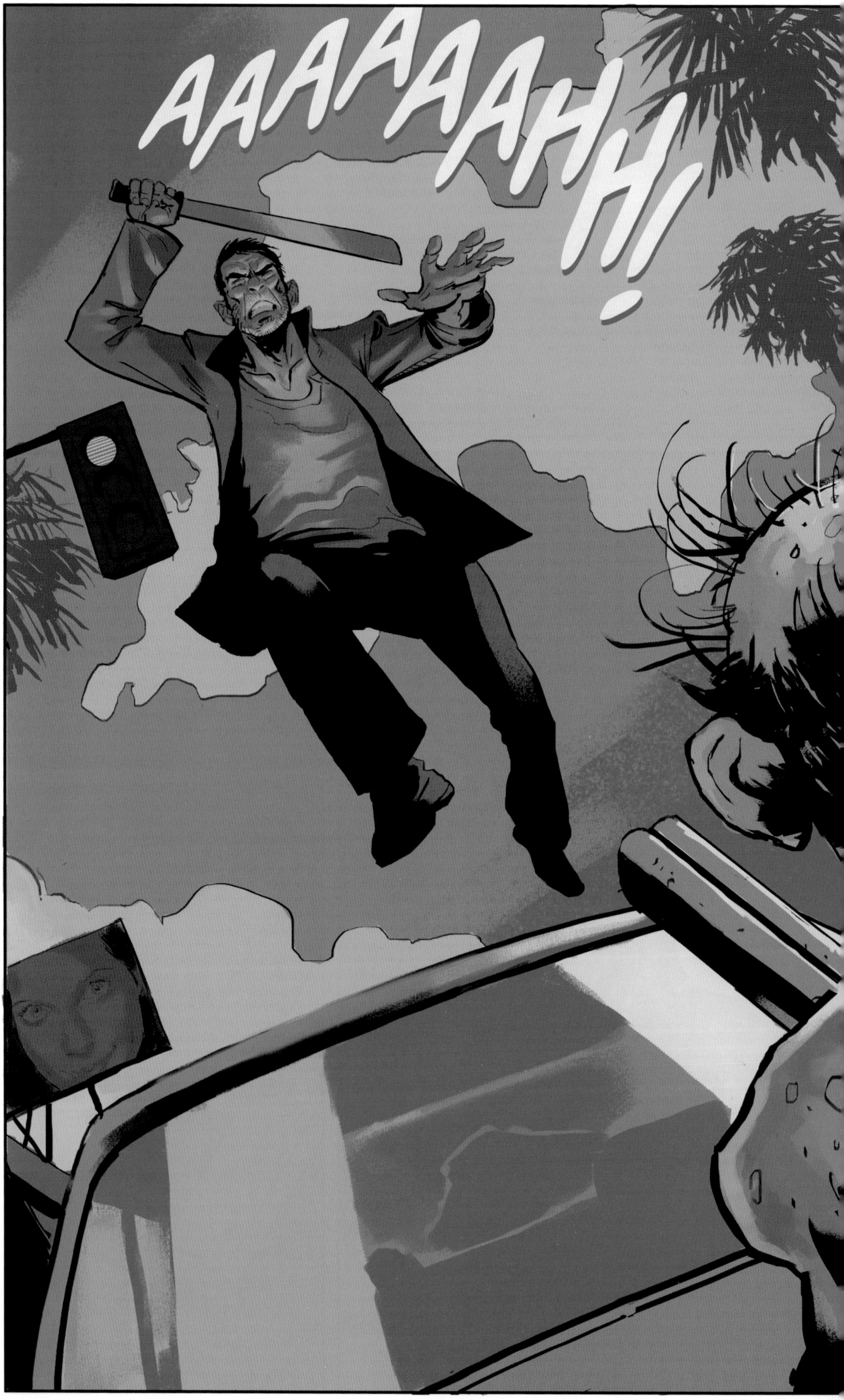
AAAAAAAHH!!

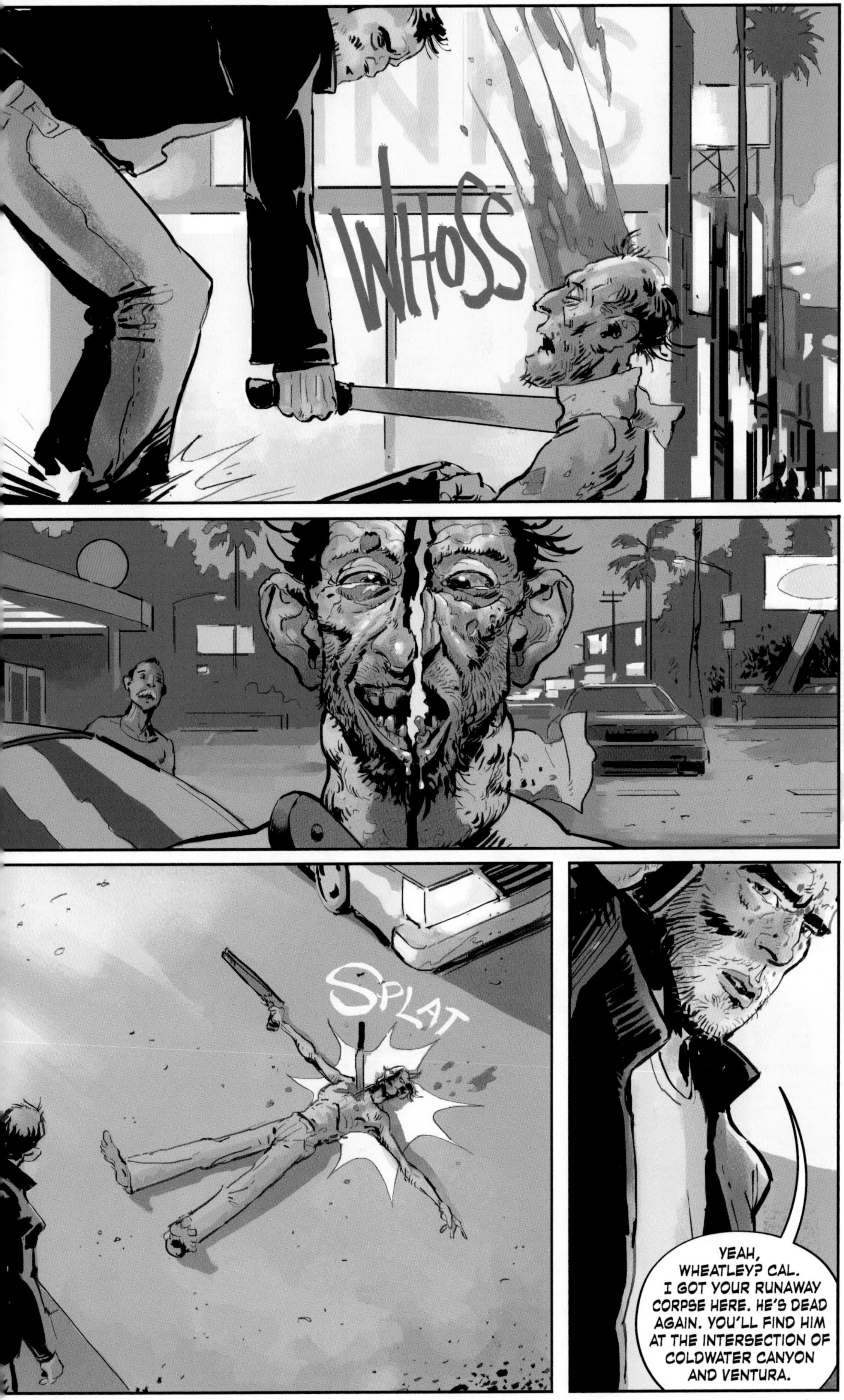
WHOSS
SPLAT
YEAH, WHEATLEY? CAL. I GOT YOUR RUNAWAY CORPSE HERE. HE'S DEAD AGAIN. YOU'LL FIND HIM AT THE INTERSECTION OF COLDWATER CANYON AND VENTURA.

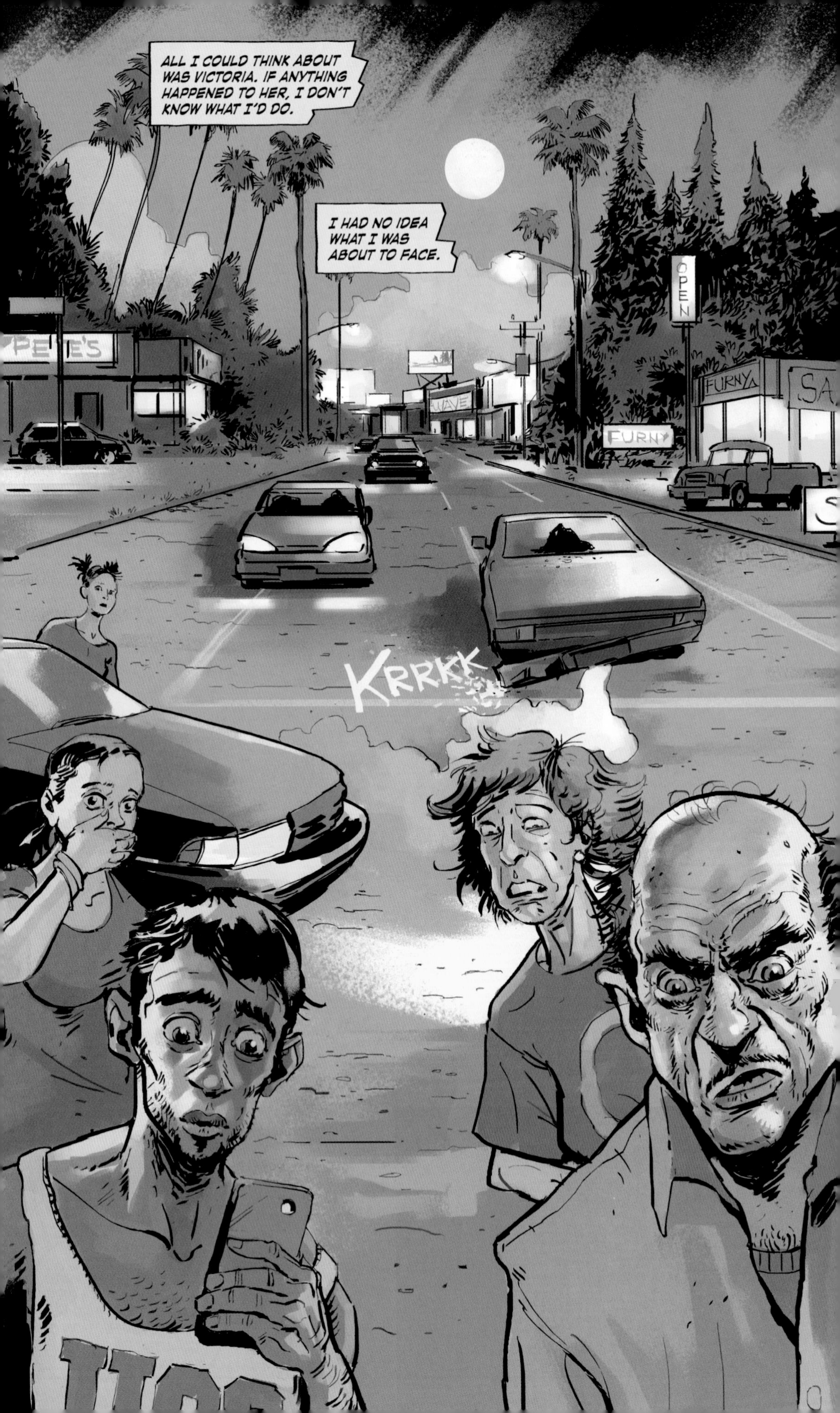
ALL I COULD THINK ABOUT WAS VICTORIA. IF ANYTHING HAPPENED TO HER, I DON'T KNOW WHAT I'D DO.
I HAD NO IDEA WHAT I WAS ABOUT TO FACE.
OPEN
FURNY
KRRKK

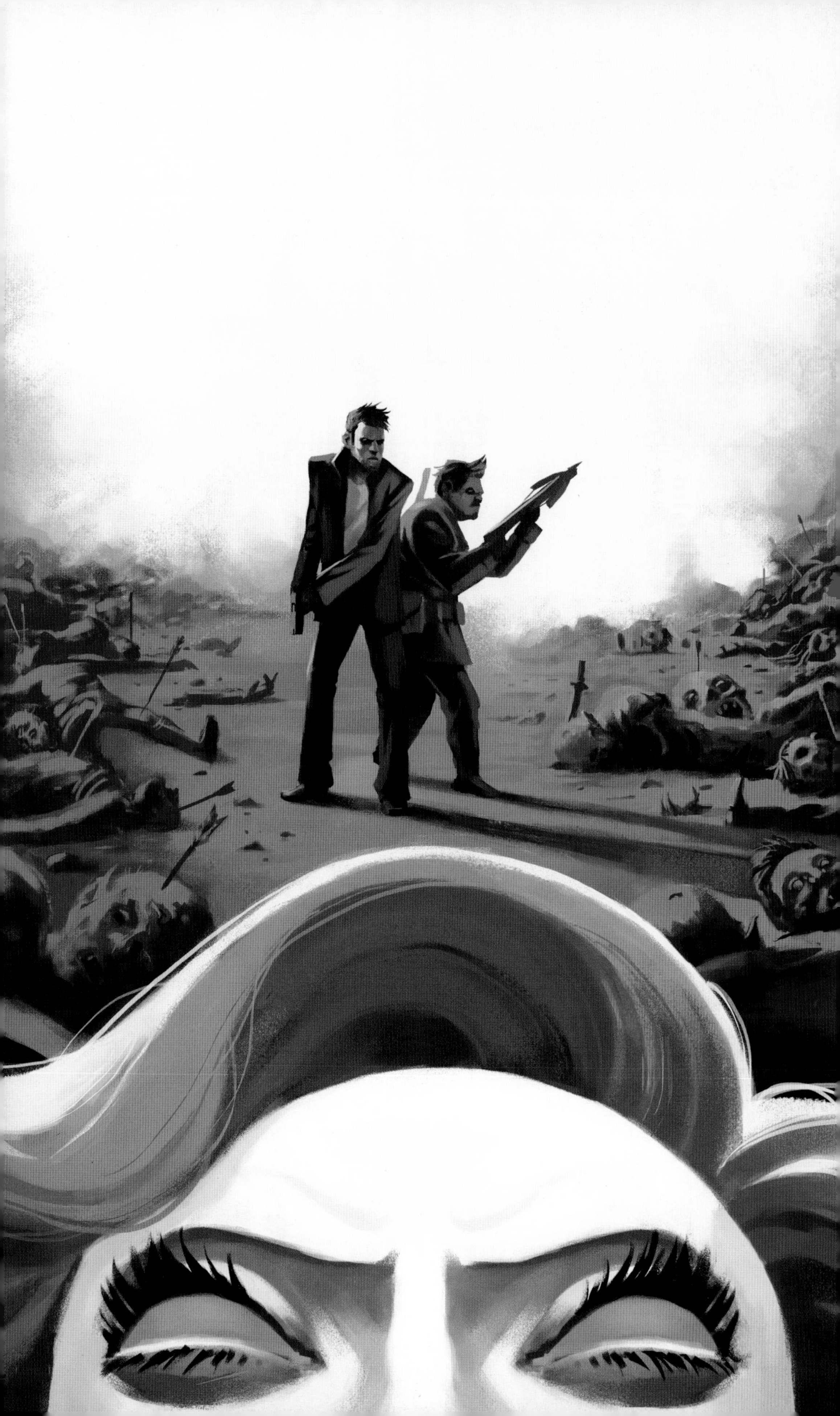

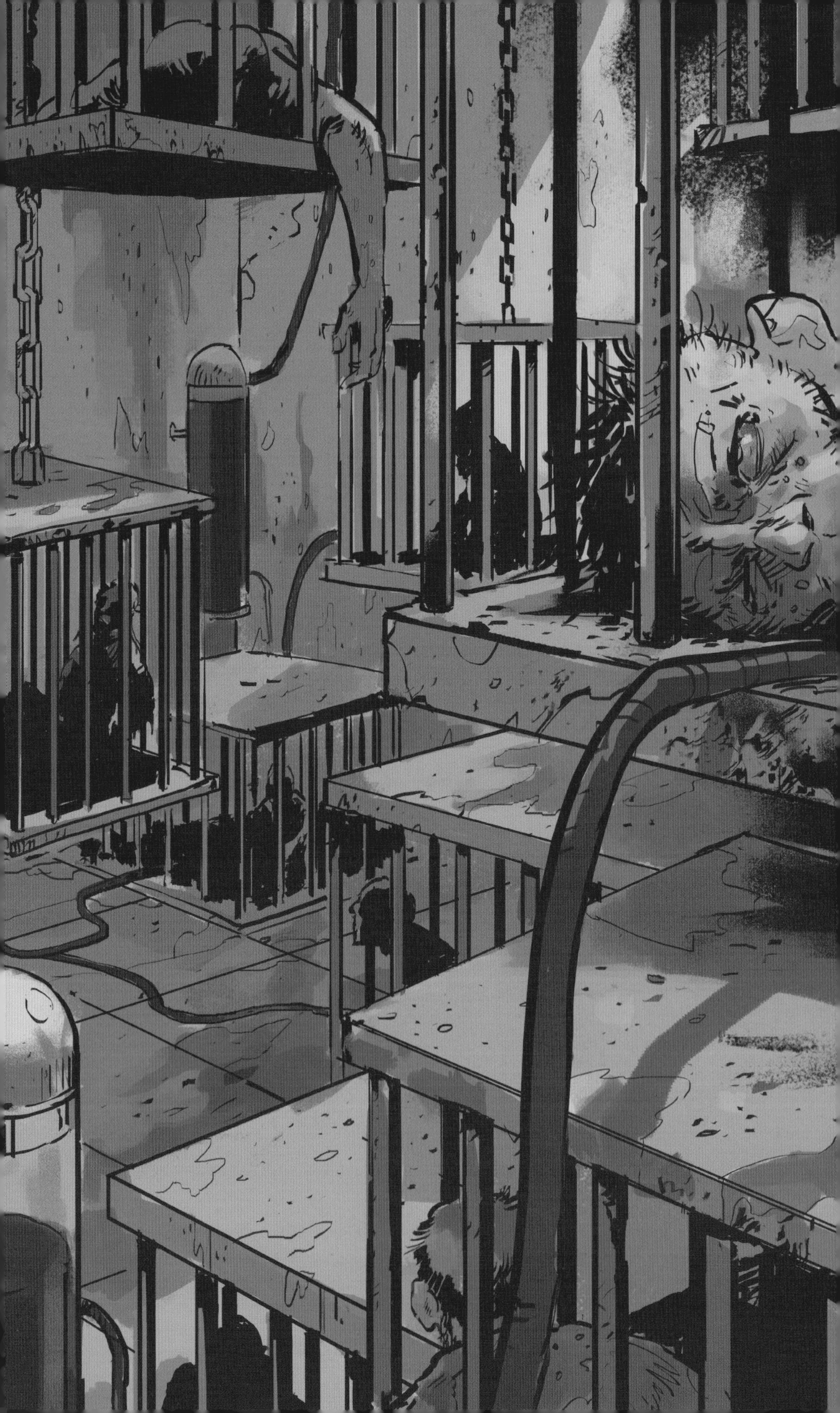

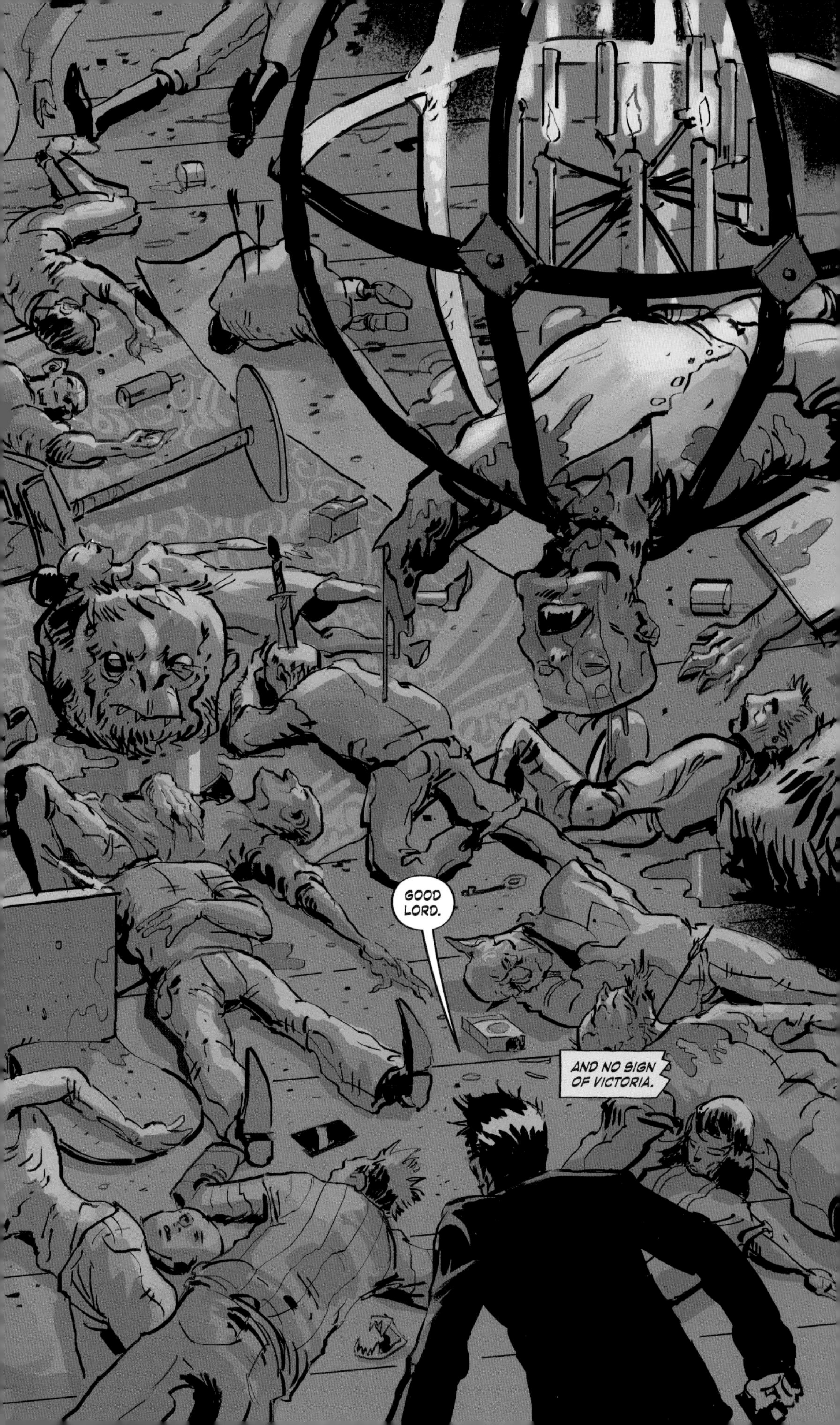
GOOD LORD.
AND NO SIGN OF VICTORIA.

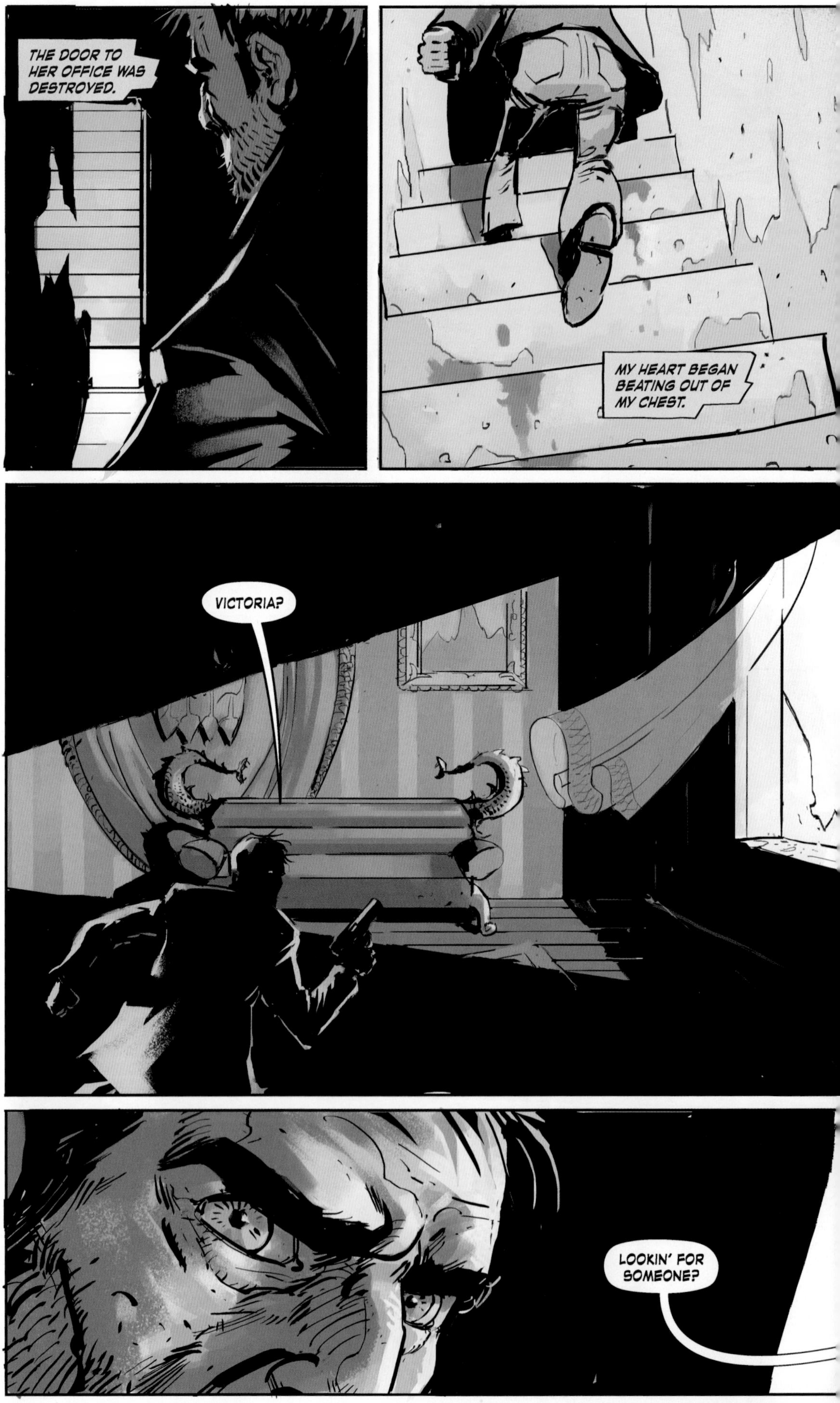
THE DOOR TO HER OFFICE WAS DESTROYED.
MY HEART BEGAN BEATING OUT OF MY CHEST.
VICTORIA?
LOOKIN' FOR SOMEONE?

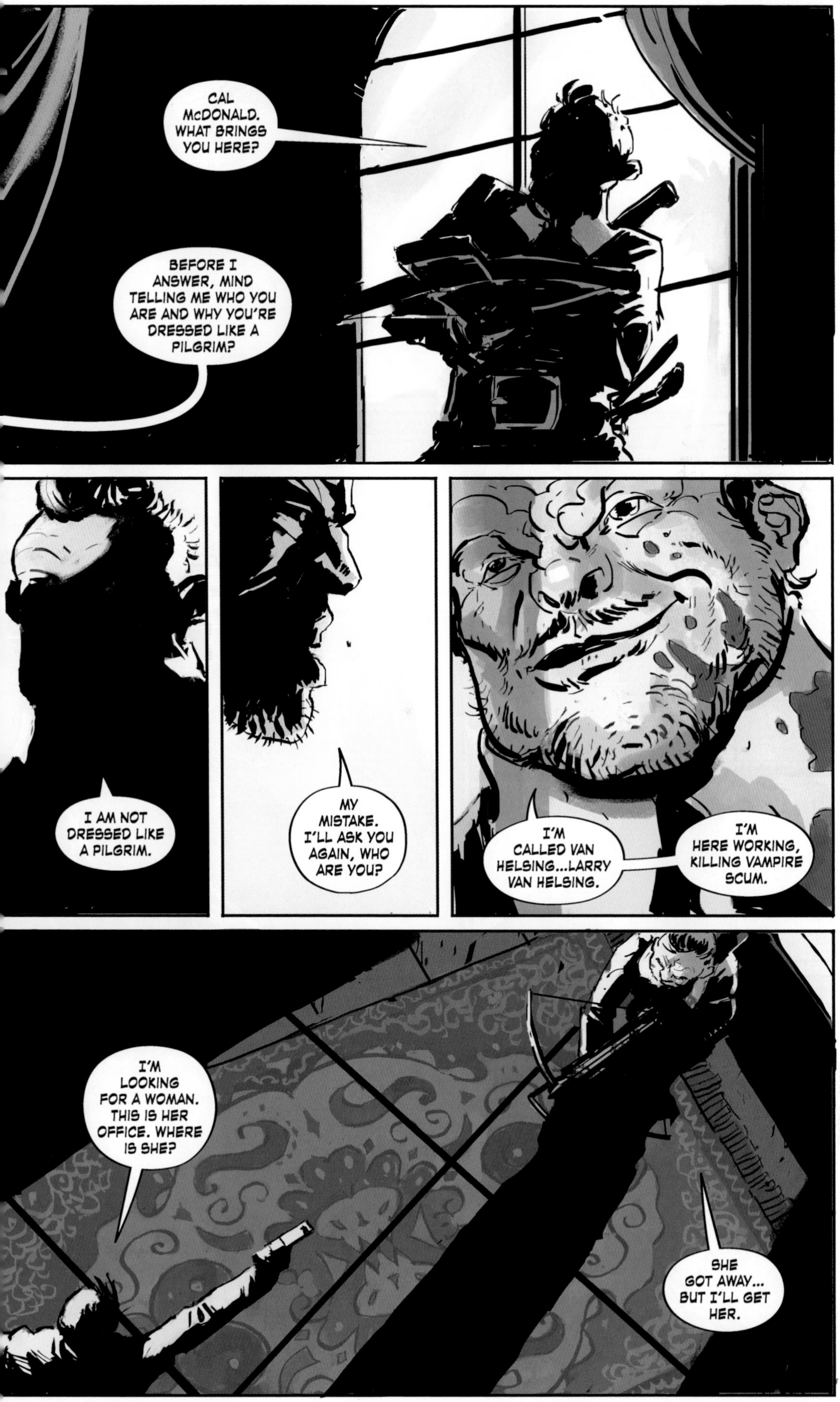
CAL McDONALD. WHAT BRINGS YOU HERE?
BEFORE I ANSWER, MIND TELLING ME WHO YOU ARE AND WHY YOU'RE DRESSED LIKE A PILGRIM?
I AM NOT DRESSED LIKE A PILGRIM.
MY MISTAKE. I'LL ASK YOU AGAIN, WHO ARE YOU?
I'M CALLED VAN HELSING...LARRY VAN HELSING.
I'M HERE WORKING, KILLING VAMPIRE SCUM.
I'M LOOKING FOR A WOMAN. THIS IS HER OFFICE. WHERE IS SHE?
SHE GOT AWAY... BUT I'LL GET HER.

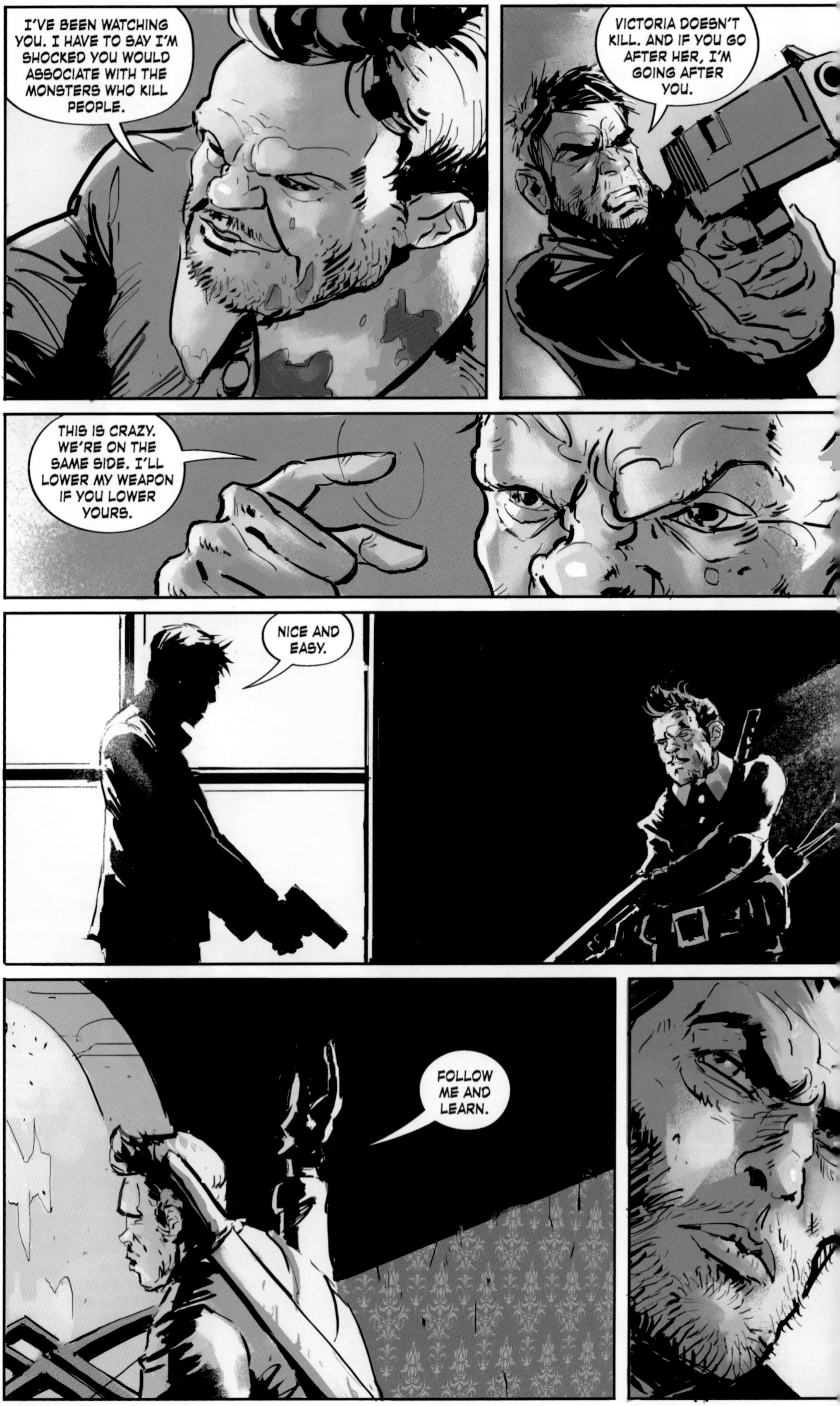
I'VE BEEN WATCHING YOU. I HAVE TO SAY I'M SHOCKED YOU WOULD ASSOCIATE WITH THE MONSTERS WHO KILL PEOPLE.
VICTORIA DOESN'T KILL. AND IF YOU GO AFTER HER, I'M GOING AFTER YOU.
THIS IS CRAZY. WE'RE ON THE SAME SIDE. I'LL LOWER MY WEAPON IF YOU LOWER YOURS.
NICE AND EASY.
FOLLOW ME AND LEARN.

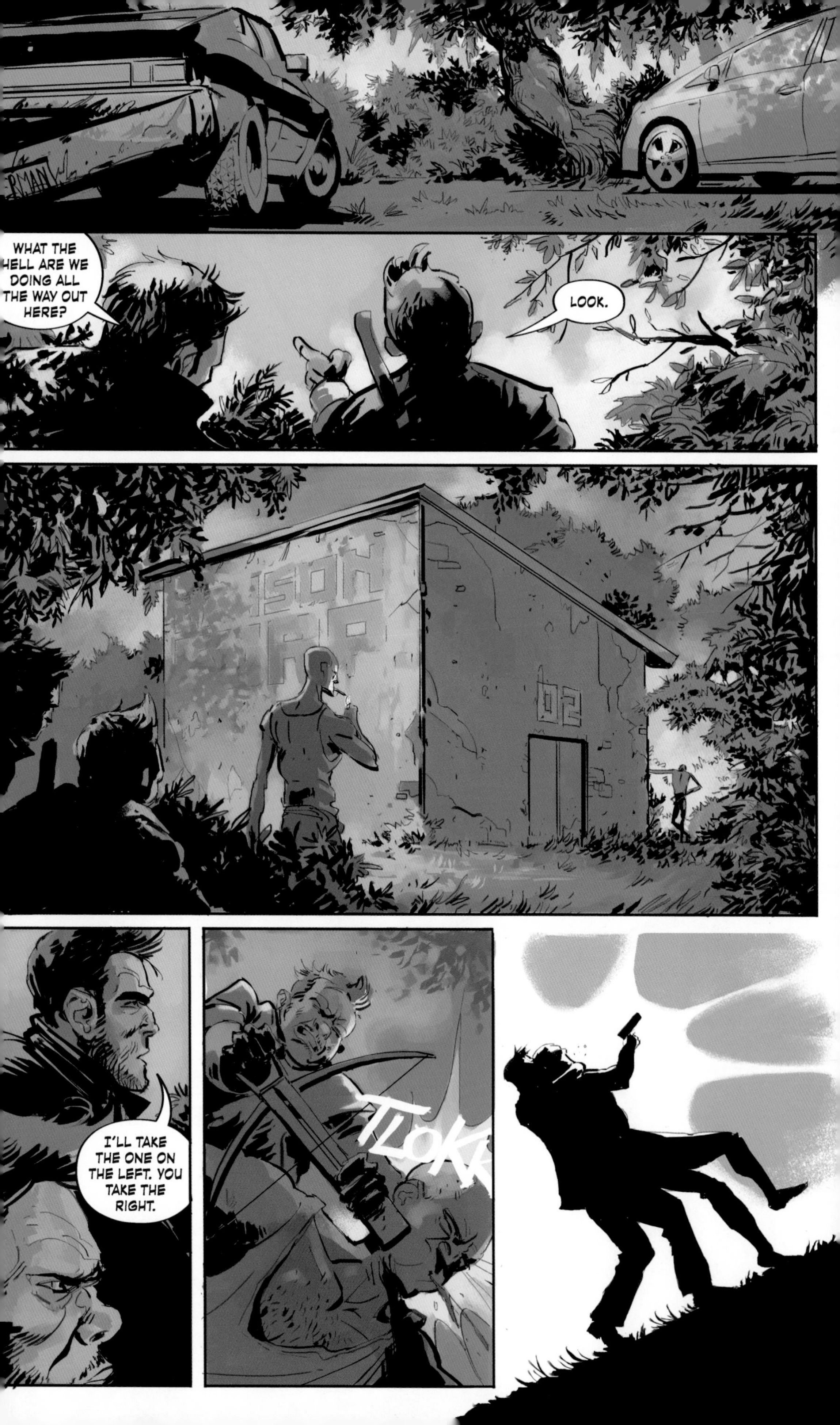

RMAN
WHAT THE HELL ARE WE DOING ALL THE WAY OUT HERE?
LOOK.
02
I'LL TAKE THE ONE ON THE LEFT. YOU TAKE THE RIGHT.
TLOKK

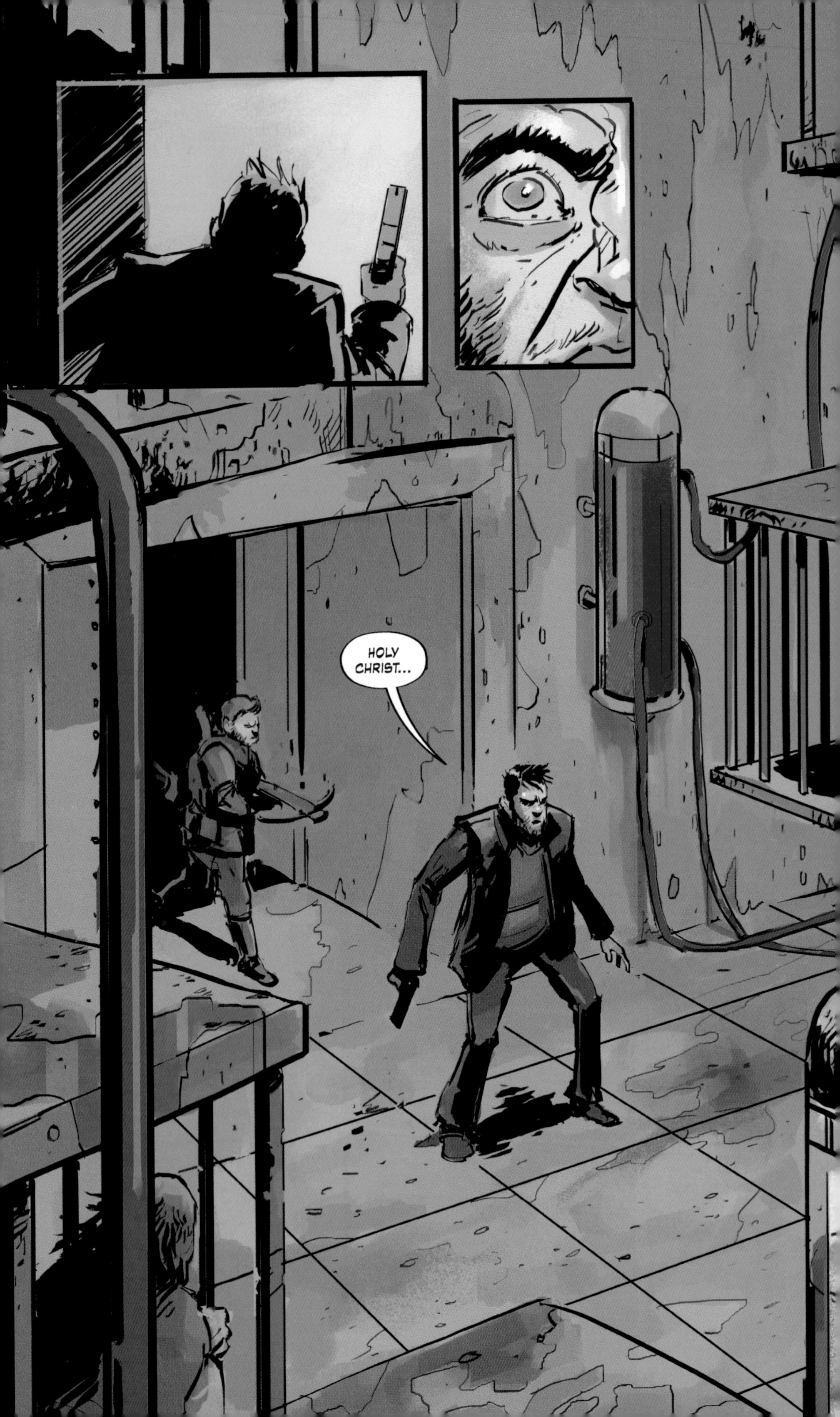
HOLY CHRIST...

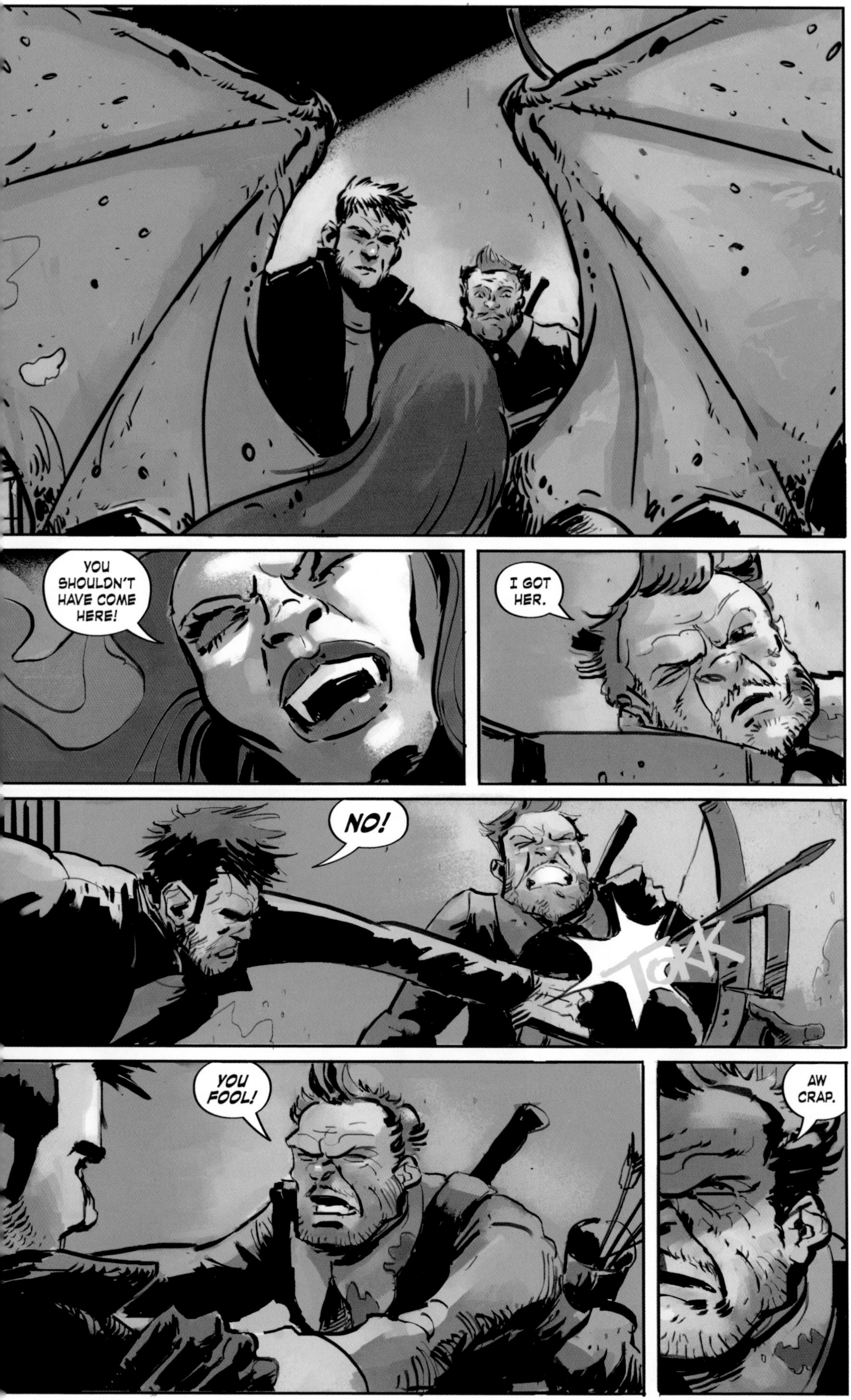

YOU SHOULDN'T HAVE COME HERE!
I GOT HER.
NO!
TOKK
YOU FOOL!
AW CRAP.

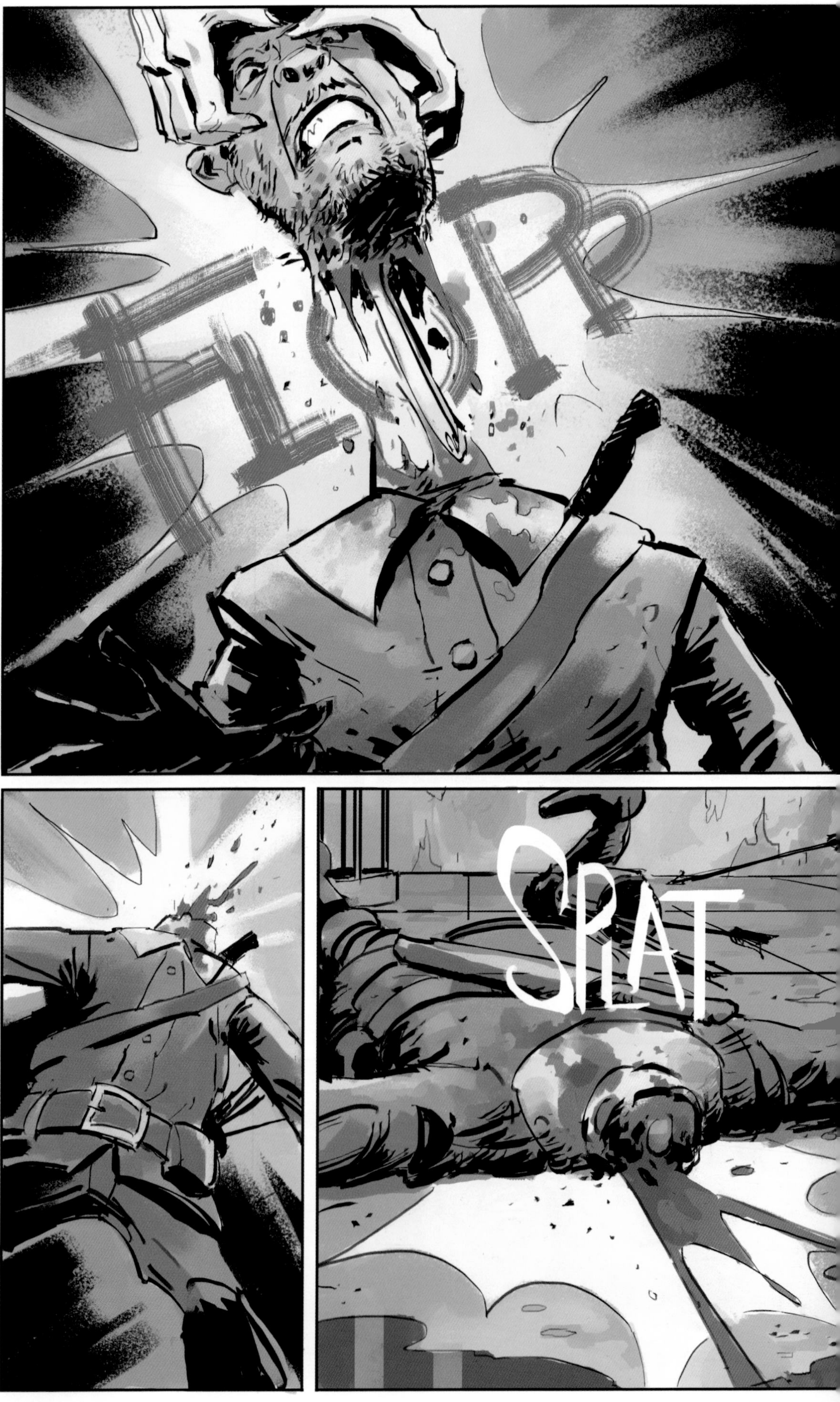
SPLAT

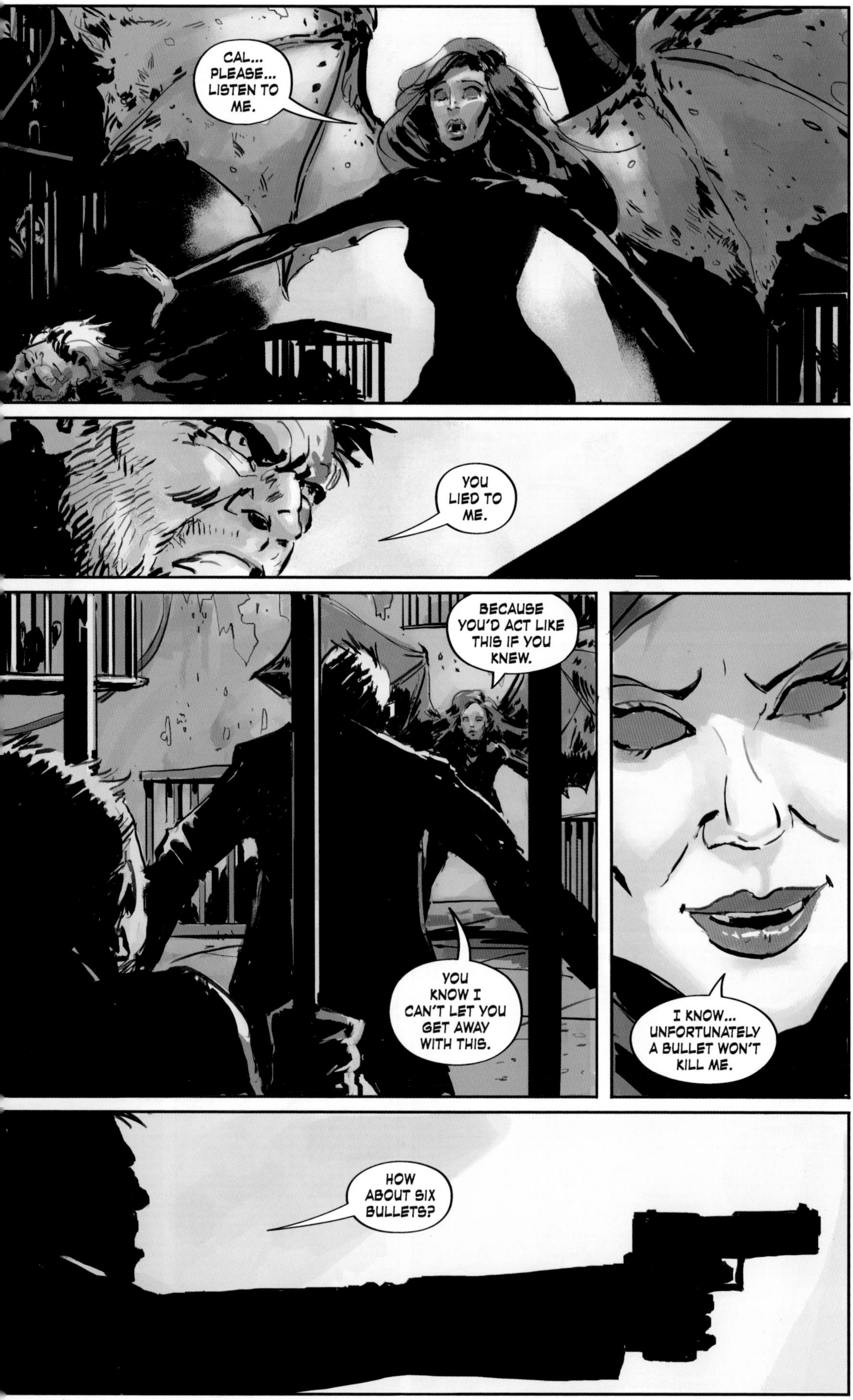
CAL... PLEASE... LISTEN TO ME.
YOU LIED TO ME.
BECAUSE YOU'D ACT LIKE THIS IF YOU KNEW.
YOU KNOW I CAN'T LET YOU GET AWAY WITH THIS.
I KNOW... UNFORTUNATELY A BULLET WON'T KILL ME.
HOW ABOUT SIX BULLETS?

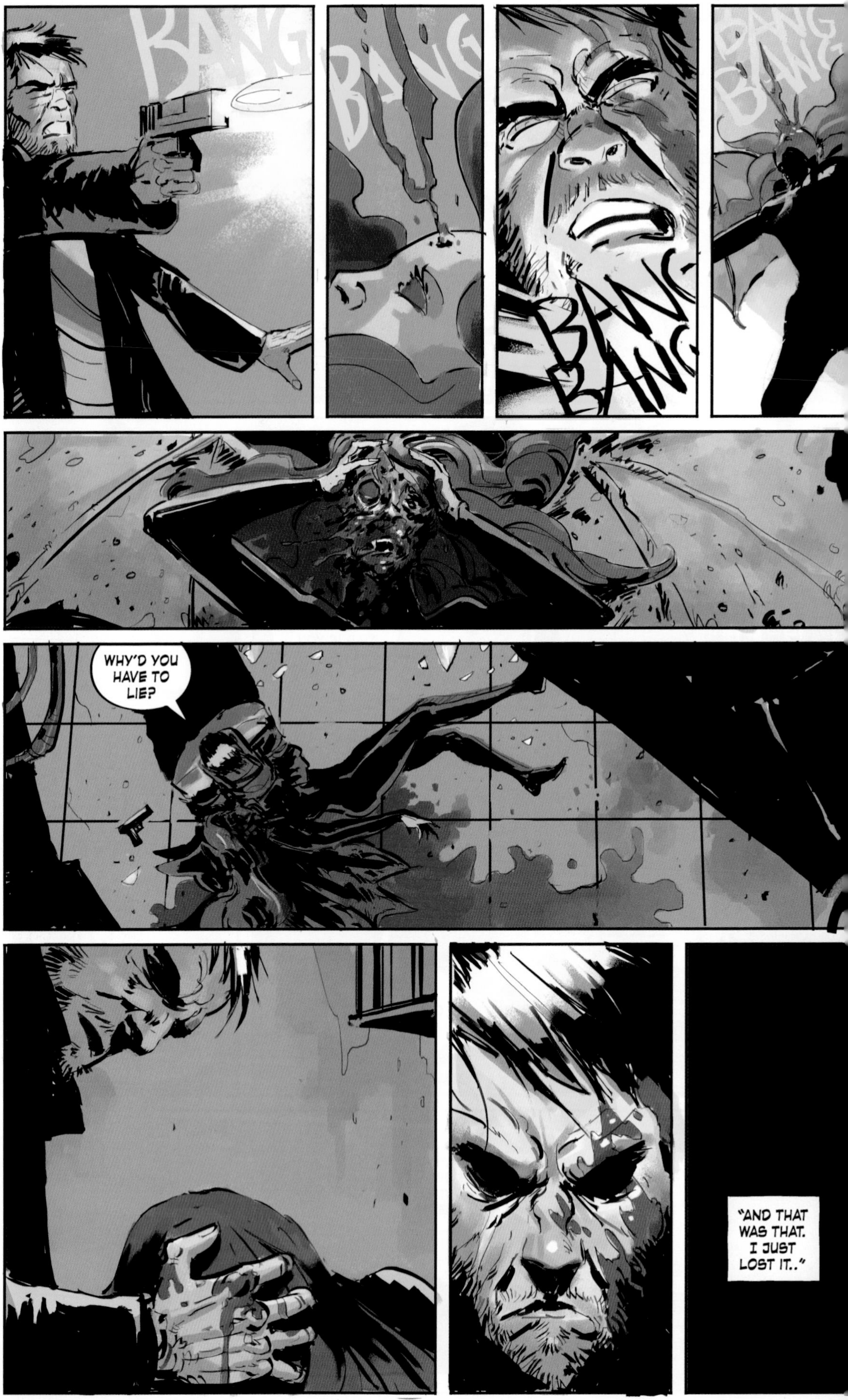
BANG
BANG
BANG
BANG
BANG
BANG
WHY'D YOU HAVE TO LIE?
"AND THAT WAS THAT. I JUST LOST IT.."

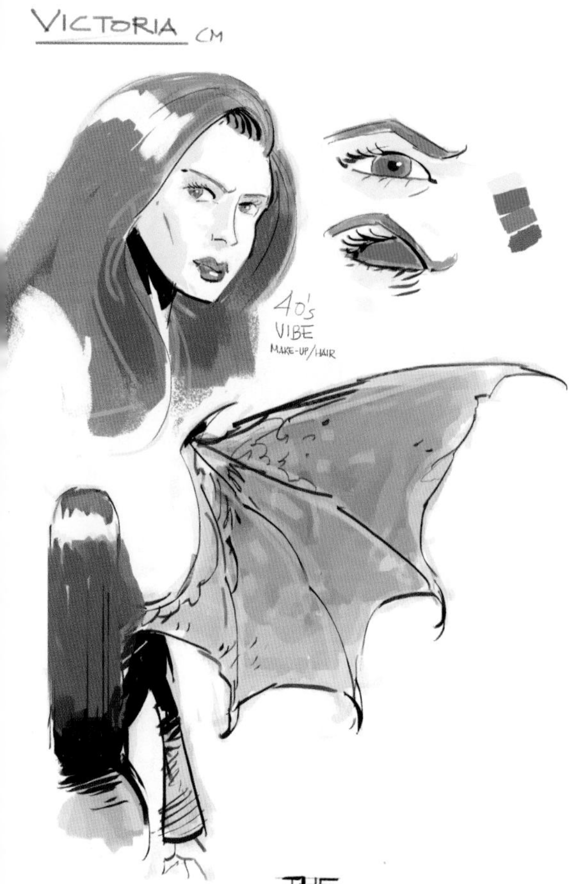
VICTORIA CM
40's
VIBE
MAKE-UP/HAIR

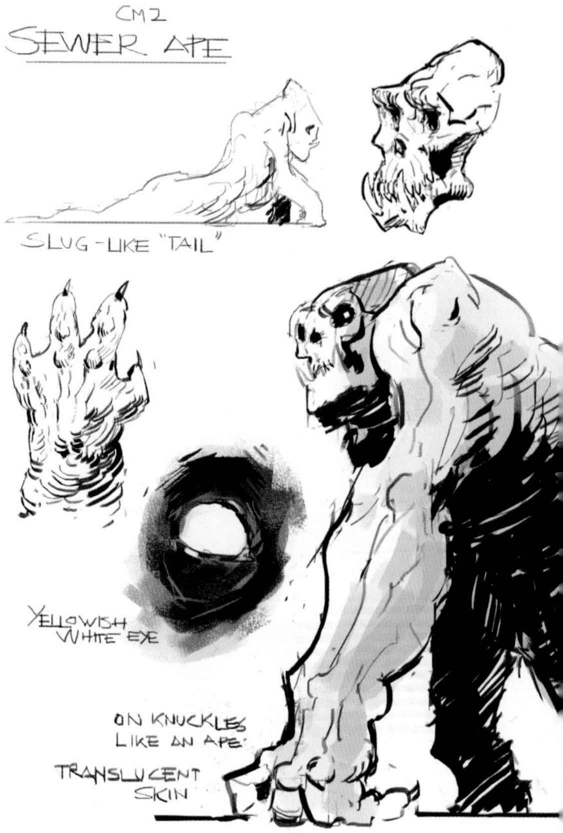
CM2
SEWER APE
SLUG-LIKE "TAIL"
YELLOWISH
WHITE EYE
ON KNUCKLES
LIKE AN APE
TRANSLUCENT
SKIN

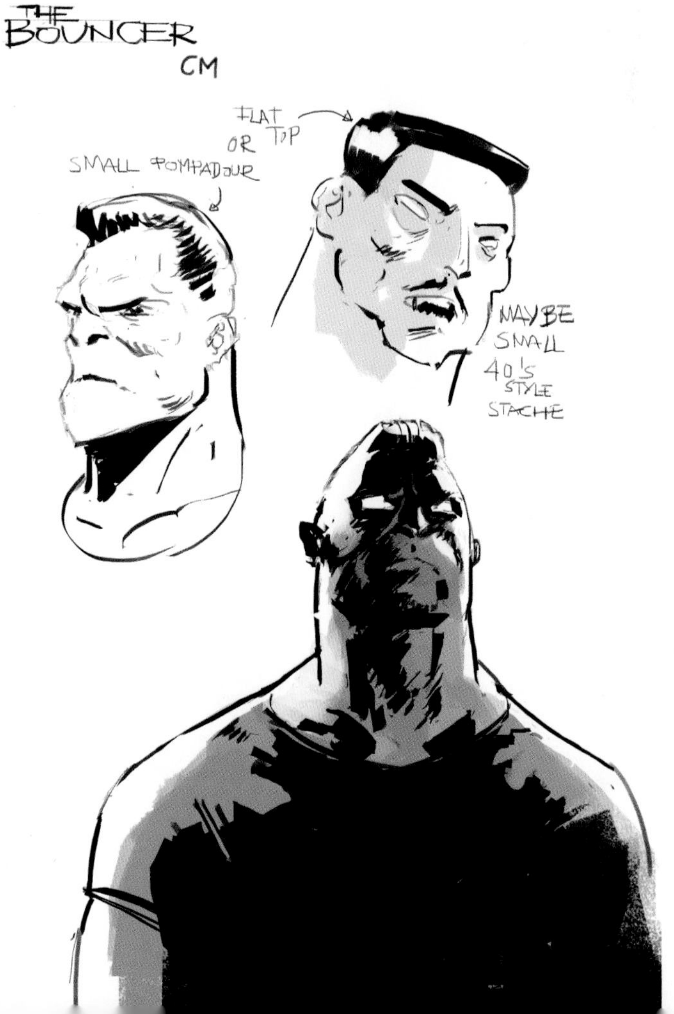
THE BOUNCER
CM
FLAT TOP
OR
SMALL POMPADOUR
MAYBE
SMALL
40's
STYLE
STACHE

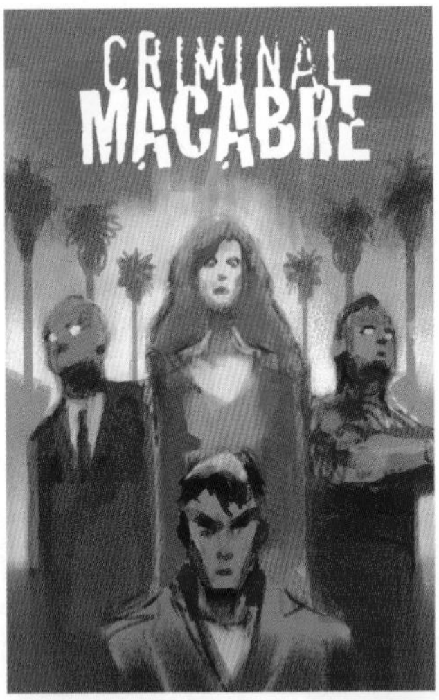
CRIMINAL
MACABRE
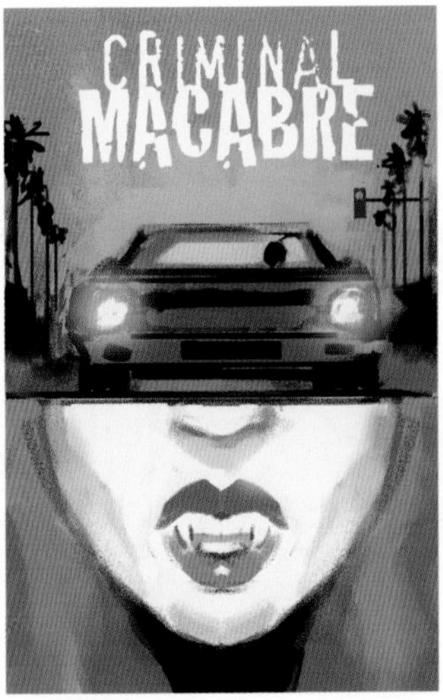
CRIMINAL
MACABRE
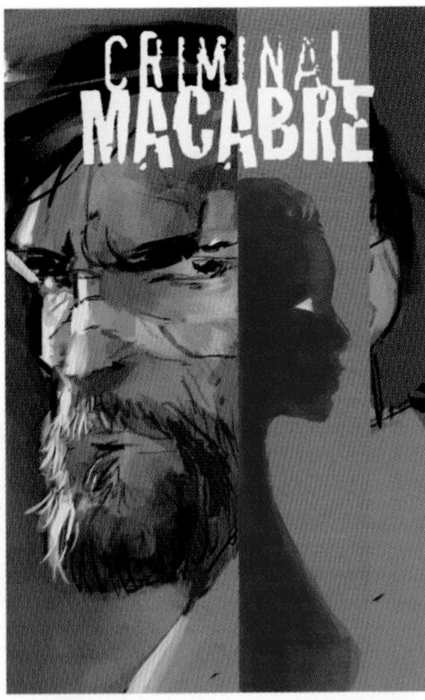
CRIMINAL
MACABRE
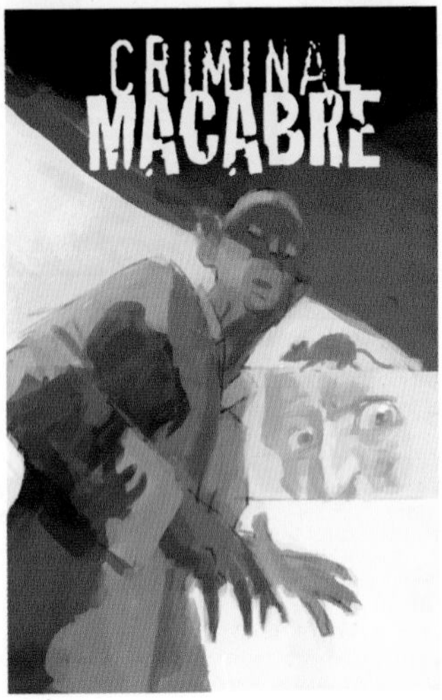
CRIMINAL
MACABRE
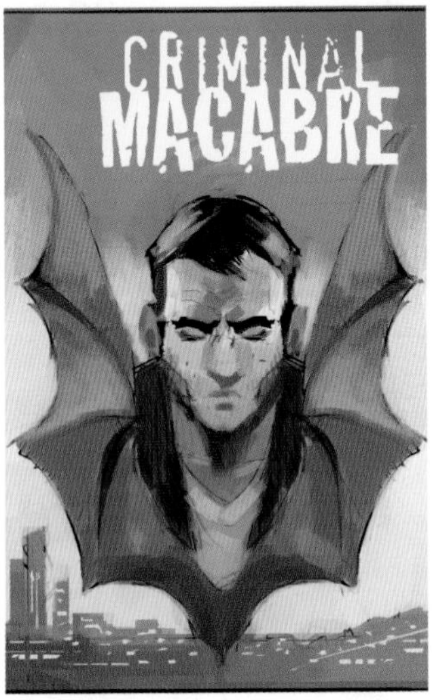
CRIMINAL
MACABRE
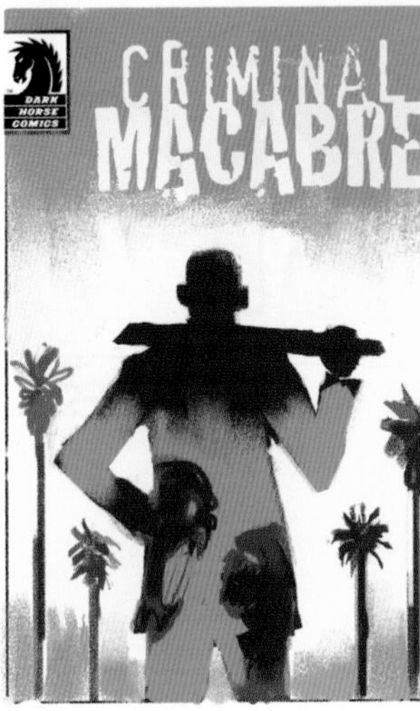
DARK HORSE COMICS
CRIMINAL
MACABRE
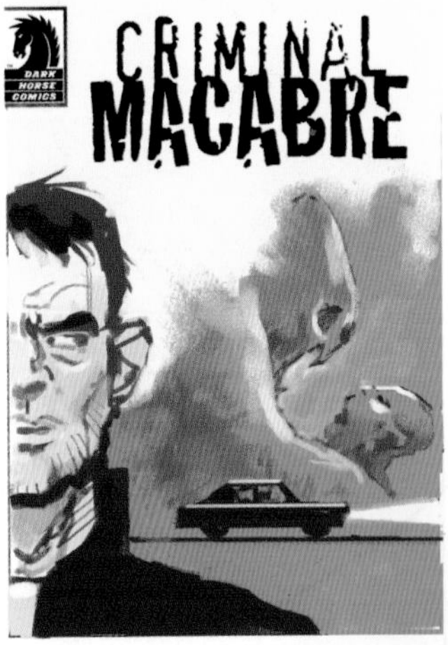
DARK HORSE COMICS
CRIMINAL
MACABRE
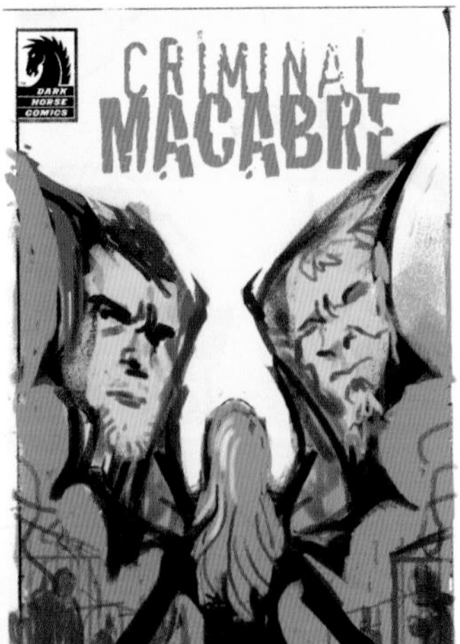
DARK HORSE COMICS
CRIMINAL
MACABRE
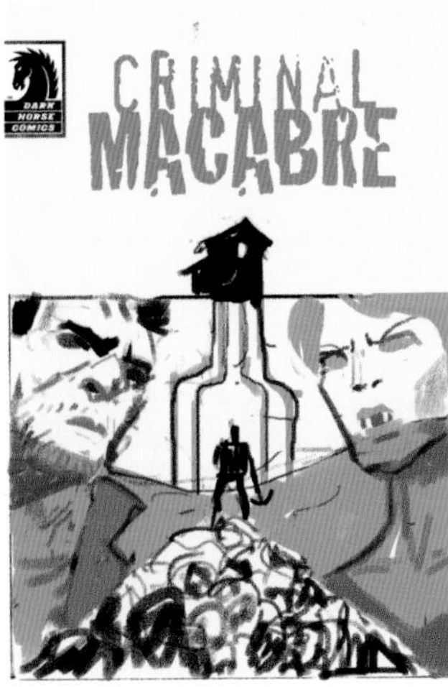
DARK HORSE COMICS
CRIMINAL
MACABRE

Cover sketches for issues 2—4.

A BRAND-NEW CAL MCDONALD MACABRE STORY

by Steve Niles (*30 Days of Night*)! A noir tale of mysteries, vampires, love, and betrayal.

Supernatural detective Cal McDonald, found wandering the streets as a disheveled vagrant, is ripped from his self-imposed retirement to resume his monster-killing career. But Cal is reluctant to return to the fray. What has the hard-bitten investigator so shaken? It's a long story that begins with a beautiful woman who happens to be a vampire . . . and ends with a bang.

"*The Big Bleed Out* [. . .] is the detective story that we need but don't deserve. It's an intelligently well-written piece of literature that pays homage to great literary works like *The Maltese Falcon* and *Red Harvest*."

—Adventures in Poor Taste

"Niles [is] one of the greatest 'monster comic' writers of the last decade."

—Bloody Disgusting

"Steve Niles [is] the king of horror comics."

—Geek Syndicate

"Niles is one of the most prolific writers, not only in horror comics, but in comics in general."

—Bloody Good Horror

Collects issues #1–#4 of the hit limited series

$19.99 US
$25.99 CAN

DarkHorse.com

DARK HORSE COMICS

ISBN 978-1-50671-536-0

51999>

9 781506 715360

FALLEN WORLD™

VALIANT®

DAN ABNETT | ADAM POLLINA | ULISES ARREOLA

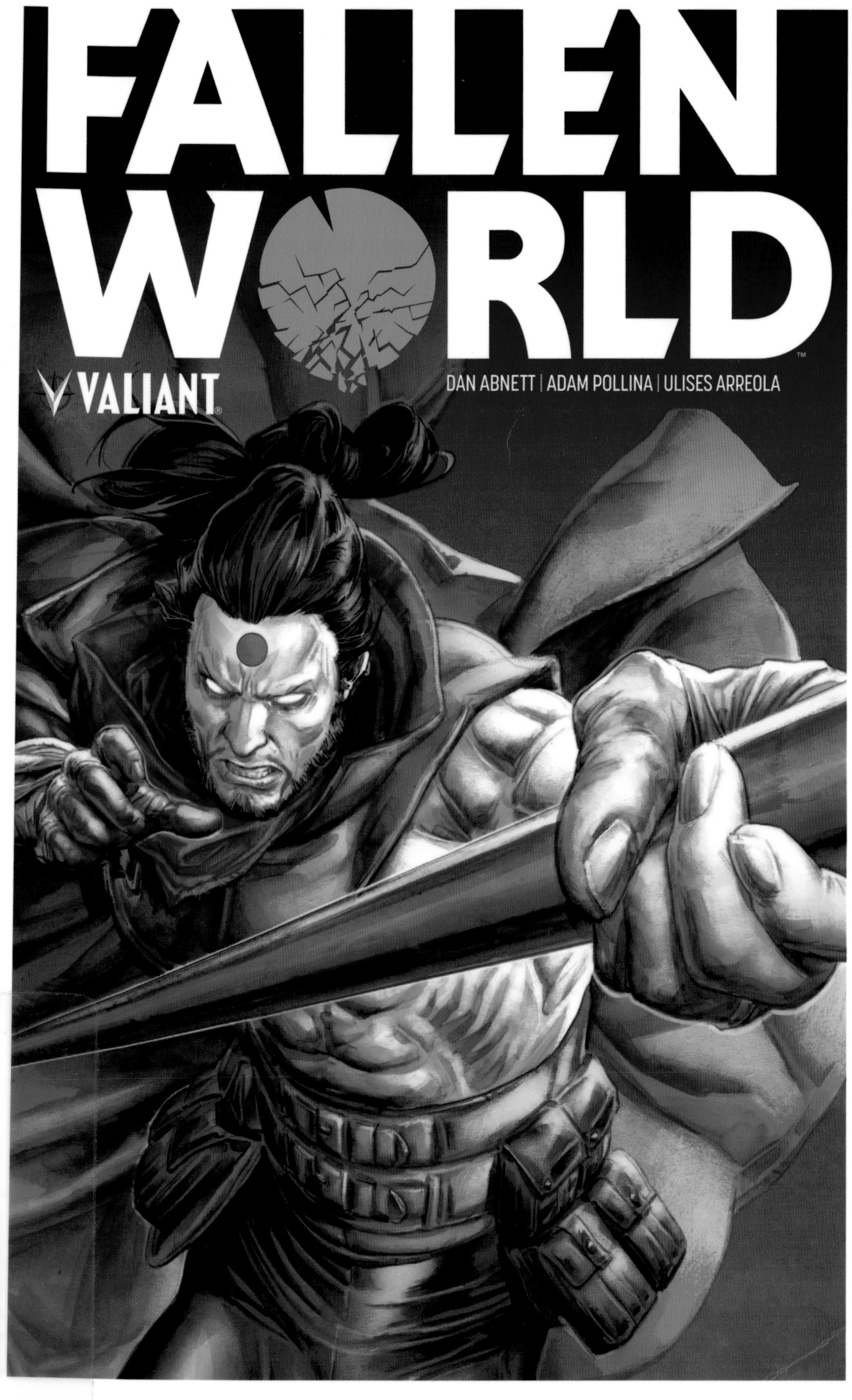